Tennessee Williams, T-s
and the Refashioning

Tennessee Williams, T-shirt Modernism and the Refashionings of Theater

S. E. Gontarski

And I will, I must and so I will
Dwell beneath the desert still
For there's no safety to be acquired
Riding streetcars named desire

—Sinéad O'Connor

ANTHEM PRESS

Anthem Press
An imprint of Wimbledon Publishing Company
www.anthempress.com

This edition first published in UK and USA 2021
by ANTHEM PRESS
75–76 Blackfriars Road, London SE1 8HA, UK
or PO Box 9779, London SW19 7ZG, UK
and
244 Madison Ave #116, New York, NY 10016, USA

British Library Cataloguing-in-Publication Data
A catalogue record for this book is available from the British Library.

ISBN-13: 978-1-78527-687-3 (Pbk)
ISBN-10: 1-78527-687-5 (Pbk)

Cover: Carl Van Vechten portrait photograph of Marlon Brando during the Broadway
production of *A Streetcar Named Desire* (December 27, 1948)

This work is from the Carl Van Vechten Photographs collection at the Library of
Congress. According to the library, there are no known copyright restrictions on
the use of this work.

This title is also available as an e-book.

For Marsha,
If not for you...

CONTENTS

List of Illustrations   ix
Acknowledgments   xi

Saint Tennessee: An Introduction   1

1. T-shirt Modernism and Performed Masculinities: The Theatrical
   Refashionings of Tennessee Williams and William Inge   9

2. "Intense Honesty": Race, Sex and Cross-Cultural Perspectives   33

3. Becoming Samuel Beckett: Tennessee Williams and Theatrical
   Change on the Post–World War II World Stage   61

4. Reframing Tennessee: A Short Afterword   85

Notes   97
Bibliography   105
Index   113

ILLUSTRATIONS

0.1 The streetcar took its name from its destination, Desire Street, in the 9th Ward of New Orleans. The street name is posted here in aging white tiles on the side of a corner building   3

1.1 Neck-to-ankle Union Suit advertised in the Sears Roebuck catalog for 1902   11

1.2 A 1904 magazine advertisement by Cooper Underwear Company   12

1.3 Advertisement in the *New Haven Leader*, New Haven, Missouri, October 16, 1919   13

1.4 Wardrobe test for film adaptation of *A Streetcar Named Desire*, August 9, 1950   14

1.5 Marlon Brando as Johnny Strabler in the 1953 American film noir crime film, directed by László Benedek, *The Wild One*   16

1.6 Tempera and oil on linen painting of one of the play's iconic scenes by American regionalist painter, Thomas Hart Benton. *Poker Night* (1948) now in the Whitney Museum's permanent collection   19

1.7 Scene from the 1951 film version of *A Streetcar Named Desire* demonstrating sharply contrasting modes of dress between Mitch (left) and Stanley (center)   19

2.1 *A Streetcar Named Desire*, first edition cover design by Alvin Lustig   36

2.2 The New Watergate Theatre Club, *Cat on a Hot Tin Roof* cast list   43

2.3 Program for *A Streetcar Named Desire*, "Directed by Laurence Olivier from the New York Production"   47

3.1 José Quintero's pre-Broadway tryout of *Clothes for a Summer Hotel* at The Kennedy Center, DC, January 1980. Poster features the passion of Zelda   71

3.2 Peter Hall's 1989 revival of *Orpheus Descending* in New York   76

3.3 Elio De Capitani's Milan revival of *Improvvisamente, l'estate scorsa* [*Suddenly, Last Summer*], 2011   77

4.1   *Endgame* by Complicité (2009) with Simon McBurney as Clov (l)
      and Mark Rylance as Hamm (r)   86
4.2   Lee Breuer's *Un tramway nommé Désir* [*A Streetcar Named Desire*] at
      the Comedie-Française, 2014   90
4.3   Lee Breuer's *Un tramway nommé Désir* [*A Streetcar Named Desire*] at
      thc Comedie-Française, 2014   92
4.4   Vinicio Marchioni as Stanley channeling Brando in Antonio
      Latella's 2011, *Un tram che si chiama Desiderio* [*A Streetcar Named
      Desire*]. Photo by Brunella Giolivo   94
4.5   Laura Marinoni as a sexually superior Blanche in Antonio
      Latella's 2011 *Un tram che si chiama Desiderio* [*A Streetcar Named
      Desire*]. Photo by Brunella Giolivo   95

ACKNOWLEDGMENTS

Much of the impetus for this extended reflection on Tennessee Williams was generated by a commission from my long-time colleague and friend, Professor Annamaria Cascetta, who asked me to edit, with critical essays on themes, style and performances, an American play that had a profound impact on what she and her co-editor called the *Canone teatrale europeo/Canon of European Drama* for their bilingual book series of that title. Given Tennessee Williams's substantial associations with Italy, the choice was obvious, and the result, *Un tram che si chiama desiderio/A Streetcar Named Desire*, appeared in 2012. Much of the work on that book was facilitated by a resident fellowship at the Bogliasco Foundation, Ligurian Study Center for the Arts and Humanities, Bogliasco, Italy, in February 2011.

Cascetta subsequently invited me to participate in a conference of invited speakers under the title "Theatre Culture, European Identity" held at the Italian Cultural Institute of New York (Italian Consulate) on September 24, 2014, at which I delivered the lecture, "Tennessee Williams and the Canon of European Theater." Cascetta subsequently organized a larger, follow-up conference in Milan entitled "IDENTITÀ EUROPEA: Diritto, storia, cultura artistica e teatrale" at her home institution, the Università Cattolica del Sacro Cuore, in May of 2017. That lecture was subsequently published in 2018 in the volume of conference papers, *European Cultural Identity: Law, History, Theatre and Art.*

Some of the material in this reassessment of Tennessee Williams's performative and critical reputation, then, has appeared in preliminary versions as follows:

"T-Shirt Modernism and the Performance of Masculinity: The Theatrical Fashionings of Tennessee Williams and William Inge," Copyright © 2020 Arizona Board of Regents. This article first appeared in *Arizona Quarterly* vol. 76, no. 4 (Winter 2020), pp. 1–28, published by Johns Hopkins University Press. My thanks to Daniel J. Crumbo, managing editor, for his attentiveness to this publication.

"Tennessee Williams's Creative Frisson, Censorship, and the Queering of Theatre" appeared in *New Theatre Quarterly* vol. 37, no. 1 (February 2021), pp. 82–99. Special thanks to Maria Shevtsova—professor of Drama and Theatre Arts at Goldsmiths, University of London, and editor of *New Theatre Quarterly* from Cambridge University Press—for her guidance, care and attention to this essay version, which she has called, "your stimulating article—really of significant importance to the present on so many counts."

"Tennessee Williams and Theatrical Change on the Post World War II World Stage" appeared in *European Cultural Identity: Law, History, Theatre and Art*, ed. Enzo Balboni and Annamaria Cascetta. Pisa: Edizioni ETS, 2018, pp. 227–43. Paper presented at the International Conference, Milan, May 11–12, 2017.

"Two Essays on Tennessee Williams" appeared in the Serbian literary journal, *Književna istorija* [*Literary History*] vol. 47, no. 156 (2015), pp. 181–210:
"*A Streetcar Named Desire*," 181–200;
"A Period of Adjustment: Zelda Fitzgerald among Tennessee's Women," 201–10.

"Zelda Fitzgerald e le donne dell' 'ultimo' Tennessee Williams," traduzione dall'inglese di Laura Peja appeared in the festschrift, *Scena Madre. Donne Personaggi E Interpreti Della Realità. Studi per Annamaria Cascetta*, a cura di Roberta Carpani, Laura Peja, Laura Aimo. Milano: Vita e Pensiero (Ricerche Media Spettacolo Processi Culturali), 2014, pp. 231–39.

"In scena" appeared in the bilingual edition *Un tram che si chiama desiderio / A Streetcar Named Desire. Canone teatrale europeo / Canon of European Drama*. No. 7. A cura di / ed. S. E. Gontarski. Pisa: Edizioni ETS, 2012, pp. 201–23.

"Per essere amati meglio morire: Williams tra censura oblio" appeared as part of a "Dossier Americani in Italia" in *Hystrio: Trimestrale di teatro e spettacolo* vol. 24, no. 4 (October–December 2011), pp. 40–41.

My thanks to the editors and publishers of these publications for their original commissions or acceptances, their editorial assessments and for permission to reprint them in revised, expanded and substantially altered versions in this volume.

SAINT TENNESSEE

An Introduction

There are three attitudes that a serious writer can adopt towards the world. He can mirror its sickness without comment; he can seek to change it; or he can withdraw from it. Mr. Williams by recommending withdrawal, places himself in the third batch, along with the saints, the hermits, the junkies and the drunks.

—Kenneth Tynan, 1957

Saint Tennessee, patron saint of the outlaw, the freak, the experimenter, the *fugitivo*? I'd pray to him.

—John Guare, 2008

He remained my patron saint.

—John Waters, 2006

Tennessee Williams emerged from obscurity and poverty suddenly, almost overnight on December 26, 1944, when the Lyric Theatre in Chicago opened *The Glass Menagerie*. That opening catapulted the impoverished, struggling writer to stardom.[1] Williams called it "a memory play," which he began working on in June of 1943 as a story about a young girl not unlike his sister Rose, with whom he was very close, who would finally undergo a highly experimental prefrontal lobotomy in 1943 to treat her worsening mental disorder. The barbaric, "ice pick" procedure designed to insure her docility left her institutionalized for the remainder of her life.[2] A rejected screenplay at MGM studios, "The Gentleman Caller," and a short story, "Portrait of a Girl in Glass" (published in 1948), featuring a glass-collecting introvert named Laura who takes refuge in repeatedly listening to old music on a 1920s Victrola, were the play's prototypes. These became, then, in subsequent years, *The Glass Menagerie*, Rose Williams transformed to the equally fragile Laura Winfield, herself the prized unicorn in her magic kingdom, her collection of glass figurines. As Williams suggests in his notes to the play, Laura (Rose) "is like a piece of her own glass collection, too exquisitely fragile to move from the shelf" (cited in the *New York Times* obituary of Rose). The story and play set the tone for a life's work that would be personal, autobiographical, and more poetical and symbolic than realistic or naturalistic. The play's staging was precedent breaking, featuring slide projections and nonrealistic, often dreamlike lighting and was finally more about memories of failed fatherhood (or parenthood) than about the failures of capitalist economics, although the latter was not without pertinence in an America still emerging from the Great Depression. The play's opening lines establish the Williams tone not only for his first success but also for his entire career, as his namesake and the play's protagonist and commentator, Tom Winfield, says: "Yes, I have tricks in my pocket, I have things up my sleeve. But I am the opposite of a stage magician. He gives you illusion that has the appearance of truth. I give you truth in the pleasant disguise of illusion." With *The Glass Menagerie* Williams would transform the space of theater into the placeless theater of memory and consciousness, a theater of imagination where a reality is not so much recorded as one where alternatives are posited.

In March of 1945, *The Glass Menagerie* moved to the Playhouse Theater on Broadway and ran for 561 performances, Williams winning the New York Drama Critics' Circle Award for his first Broadway venture. Williams publicly evaluated his transition on the eve of *A Streetcar Named Desire*'s New York opening in an essay for the "Drama" section of the *New York Times* (November 30, 1947) called "On A Streetcar Named Success" (reprinted as "The Catastrophe of Success") as "an event that terminated one part of my life and began another"; "I was snatched out of virtual oblivion and thrust into sudden prominence," he continued, as he moved from "furnished rooms about the country [...] to a suite in a first-class Manhattan hotel." The play to follow *The Glass Menagerie* would be even more successful, more stunning, more transformative, more surprising. James Fisher notes that "Williams was the theatre's angel of sexuality—the dramatist most responsible for forcefully introducing sexual issues, both gay and straight, to the American stage" (Fisher, 1995, 13).

Sexuality was not exactly absent from the American stage in 1947, however. By the 1930s the staged variety shows of burlesque, a form of parody that featured ribald comedy and nudity, often mocking the conventions of performance, usually those of other well-known works, shifted their focus from the modestly risqué to full-out striptease.[3] Amid considerable moral resistance, such variety entertainments were sublimated into shows like the *Ziegfeld Follies* featuring, alternately and more acceptably, leggy chorus girls, a mainstay of Broadway musicals and many period Hollywood films. In 1937 the MGM production, *The Great Ziegfeld*, won the Academy Award for best

Figure 0.1 The streetcar took its name from its destination, Desire Street, in the 9th Ward of New Orleans. The street name is posted here in aging white tiles on the side of a corner building

picture. A decade later, but only a year after MGM's follow-up, star-studded film *Ziegfeld Follies* (1946), Williams would introduce images not of the female form, which today we tend to see as part of the objectification of women, nor of women as decorative teases exposing all but the most socially forbidden details of their anatomies, but of desire, most dramatically of female desire.

While male desire is the dominant thread that leads to the climactic, catastrophic rape of Blanche DuBois at the conclusion of *A Streetcar Named Desire*, much of the play is built on a substructure of female desire as the DuBois sisters pursue contrasting paths to their sexual obsessions and the fulfillment of their desires. The backstory of Blanche's sexuality is exposed by Stanley after he has friends probe Blanche's life in her native Laurel, Mississippi. But Blanche herself reveals the first act of that story, her love for Allan Grey, a like-minded, sensitive, poetically inclined youth, who finally betrays her with an extramarital affair—with a male friend. When the British censors objected to such revelations, it was not to the issue of adultery per se but to the liaison with another male. What Stanley brings to light are Blanche's coping mechanisms after the suicide of her husband, but as shocking as her flagrant sexuality is her abuse of power as a schoolteacher seducing her students, avatars of her lost husband. That is, Blanche's desire is fundamentally narcissistic. She pursues partners most like herself, in her own self-image, love objects who mirror her delicacy, sophistication, tenderness and her perceived, perpetual youthfulness. Stella's sexual desires are detailed only in the present, however. We see very little of her memory play, the path that led her from Laurel, Mississippi to her liaison with a testosterone-charged, T-shirt-wearing, working-class partner for whose affections she will finally betray her sister. What is not disclosed is Stella's sweet bird of youth. She is the most radical of Williams's *Streetcar* characters, akin to the fugitive kind, someone who, like Chance Wayne, fled the restrictions of small town, Southern life with its narrow possibilities for a larger world. As Wayne suggests in *Sweet Bird of Youth* (1959),

> The great difference between people in this world is not between the rich and the poor or the good and the evil, the biggest of all differences in this world is between the ones that had or have the pleasure in love and those that haven't and hadn't any pleasure in love, but just watched it with envy, sick envy. (54)

Wayne's comment suggests the key difference between the DuBois sisters, and such are the issues of love and sexuality that Williams "forced," to adopt Fisher's term, onto the American and finally the world stage in 1947, in the aftermath of World War II, and continued to dramatize over the next decade and a half. Re-gendered, Brick Pollitt expresses a parallel vision of love in *Cat on a Hot Tin Roof* thus: "Why can't exceptional friendship, *real, real, deep, deep friendship!* Between two men be respected as something clean and decent without being thought of as [...]-- Fairies...." (64; italics in original), the last a reference to Jack Straw and Peter Ochello, the homosexual couple from whom Big Daddy inherited the property and in whose former bedroom Maggie and Brick spend their nights (and most of the play).[4] It is a conversation in which Brick's tentative, uncertain masculinity is sounded against Big Daddy's hypermasculinity. These are people formed and shaped by their desires and obsessions, riding the *Streetcar Named Desire* to the end of the line. And such revelations shaped audience and critical expectations that Williams would finally thwart in mid-career in favor of what he too, a fugitive kind, would see as a larger world, one inhabited by playwrights like Samuel Beckett and Harold Pinter, as he moved beyond what is here called "T-shirt Modernism" to more self-reflexive theater, theater that turns back on itself like an ouroboros.

Thomas Lanier Williams was born in Columbus, Mississippi, on March 26, 1911, lived for several years in Clarksdale, Mississippi, before moving with his family to St. Louis in 1918. Because of his southern accent he was called Tennessee, a name he subsequently adopted formally. His maternal grandfather, Walter E. Dakin, was an Episcopal minister, who studied theology at the University of the South, but his father was a violent alcoholic who often mocked his son's more effeminate behavior by calling him "Miss Nancy." The hard-drinking, bombastic, womanizing Cornelius Coffin Williams, who was prone to gambling, was a salesman by vocation, and who, in a line from the very autobiographical *The Glass Menagerie*, which focused on his early years in

St. Louis, "fell in love with long distances"; that is, he abandoned his family. He is thus the absent presence of *The Glass Menagerie*, more present in memory than he had ever been in the physical life of the family. His son attended a succession of universities through the years of economic depression, from 1929–38, but his education was frequently interrupted, in part due to work in the International Shoe Company in St. Louis. While the experience was emotionally debilitating and constricting for Tom, it formed the basis of what would become *The Glass Menagerie*. Williams would finally graduate from the University of Iowa in 1938, where he completed his first play, *Spring Storm*, and set about trying to become a writer on the eve of the Second World War. A $1,000 grant from the Rockefeller Foundation in 1939 (the letter arrived on December 21), as part of the foundation's support of the Authors League of America (and subsequently the National Theater Conference), allowed Williams to leave St. Louis and return to New York to concentrate on his writing. There he was subsequently invited by John Gassner to join his playwriting seminars at the New School of Social Research, which staged first *The Long Goodby* and in 1942 *This Property Is Condemned*. Growing more professional, he hired Audrey Wood as his agent.

The grant came as Williams was in dire economic straits, as he described in a letter to Luise M. Sillcox, executive secretary of the Dramatists' Guild, which administered the grants, sent on July 8, 1940, from Provincetown, Massachusetts, on what Williams called, "the frolicksome tip of Cape Cod" (*Memoirs* 53), where he most likely had his first homosexual relationship, to report on his use of the Rockefeller Foundation funds:

> I welcome the opportunity to tell you, with the limited capacity of words, something about my feelings about the Rockefeller Foundation's dramatic awards. In my case the award was particularly "dramatic." You may recall something of my situation when the award was given. I had actually hocked my typewriter, my fraternity pin, and almost everything else of negotiable value. I was at the nadir of my resources, physical, mental, spiritual. Being told about my "possibilities" no longer encouraged me. I had heard it too often—so often that I was beginning to think it would make me a damned good epitaph some day! I had written the first draft of a new play, "Battle of Angels," but I am not ashamed to say that the shock of it, coming upon a long period of terrific strain, unnerved me so that I could not get out of bed—or stop laughing and crying—for an hour or two!
>
> Since then I have finished my play—sold it to the Theatre Guild— written a new one and conceived yet another and my life contains a

completely new vista of creative work and fulfillment. I am [reasonably] happy and well adjusted and glad to be alive. (*Selected Letters*, 2002, 257)

The joy and adjustment were apparently short-lived. The Theatre Guild went on to produce the *Battle of Angels* in Boston, Massachusetts, in 1940, but it was a total failure after the New England Watch and Ward Society (originally the New England Society for the Suppression of Vice) banned the play, and the Guild refused to bring it to New York. The Watch and Ward Society's actions gave rise to the catch phrase "Banned in Boston," as Williams was, the first of his many conflicts with American and European moral censorship. Such response was not unanticipated, however, as Williams wrote to The Theater Guild's Lawrence Langner on July 2, 1940, when Joan Crawford was proposed as the lead for *Battle of Angels*, a possibility about which Williams was suspicious:

To be quite honest I regard it as an act of God that Miss Crawford did not find it suitable, though her criticism of the play as "low and common" is not within my little comprehension. Certainly the play is mainly a study of sexual passion, but serious rather than titillating, so I don't believe that any responsible critic would find any validity in such a charge. (*Selected Letters*, 2002, 258)

Williams would of course rebound from less than "responsible" critics and from being "Banned in Boston." He would eventually rewrite *Battle of Angels* as *Orpheus Descending* in 1957, but more immediately, he would go on to produce a pair of masterpieces, canonical works in the international repertory, works that, as the Harry Ransom Humanities Research Center at the University of Texas, one of the primary archives of Williams's work, characterizes them, "reinvented the American theater," *The Glass Menagerie*, shortly thereafter, and *A Streetcar Named Desire* three years after that. But the three plays are intimately interconnected in something of a Southern trilogy as Williams originally conceived the project in 1939, as *Battle of Angels* stands behind the two greater plays, they and the character of Blanche Dubois, developed from the original Irene, growing out of it and a proposed novel called *Americans*. The catalogue of the centenary exhibition at the Harry Ransom Research Center, *Becoming Tennessee Williams* (February 1–July 31, 2011), concludes that "there is no more influential 20th-century American playwright than Tennessee Williams." Charlotte Canning, curator of the exhibition and professor in the Department of Theater and Dance at the University of Texas at Austin, went on to say that "he inspired future generations of writers as diverse as Suzan-Lori Parks, Tony Kushner, David Mamet and John Waters, and his plays remain among the most produced in the world."

Of *A Streetcar Named Desire* in particular, critic Philip C. Kolin has said that it is "one of the most influential plays in the twentieth century," and such an assessment should not be restricted to the United States or even to the English-speaking world. *A Streetcar Named Desire* made an immediate and profound impact on a Europe devastated by the Second World War, as much of the continent emerged from beneath the heavy boots of Fascism. For Europe, *A Streetcar Named Desire* was of a piece with liberation, with political liberation, with literary liberation into new forms of expression and with sexual emancipation. *A Streetcar Named Desire* suggested for many a new and more open way to live, and offered for writers a set of new possibilities for their art. And while the more sensational Williams may have helped attract large theater and, finally, film audiences, his legacy as arguably the greatest and most enduring of American dramatists will rest on his language, his "intense honesty" in portraying not only human emotion and desire but also the capacities of love irrespective of gender, and on his poeticized theater, for, after all, as Williams himself has said of his work, "treatment is everything in a play of this type" and that "Chekhov takes precedence as an influence."

This study refocuses the work of Tennessee Williams against the larger fabric of cultural change in the post–World War II era in which he came to prominence, an era in which the rate of cultural change accelerated unprecedentedly into periods of fragmentation and dislocation, a cultural unmooring we now generally (if too loosely) call postmodern, or, more accurately, perhaps, late modern. The study comes to grips with the Williams we thought we knew, as he grew, developed and reconfigured himself into a playwright we didn't, in his attempts to refashion himself amid the vortices of changing sexual mores, including the redrafting of masculinities and the queering of theater, the struggle for a literate, literary theater and the place of the theatrical experience in contemporary culture.

This study, thus, continues and extends the reappraisal of Tennessee Williams to counter the received wisdom that his work fell into precipitous decline in the 1960s as the naturalism he was associated with, not always through his own choosing, was replaced by more European, meta-theatrical innovation and experimentation—and as culture saw dynamic recalibrations of sexual desire and its mores. It suggests, instead, that Williams was always experimental, always more lyrically Chekhov than realistically Ibsen, more interior than exterior, a poetic playwright inflected with the ethos of Harte Crane, and that the late and more experimental of his plays are as central to his reshaping of American theater as those works of the immediate post–World War II era that brought him fame and fortune. (See, e.g., his late, overt embrace of Chekhov, *The Notebook of Trigorin: A Free Adaptation of Chekhov's "The Seagull"*). The purpose of this study, then, is to "refocus" Williams's work in two phases: first, to demonstrate how his early, best-known works were ahead of their time in grappling with modernist understanding of "masculinities" and of queer sexualities; second, to demonstrate that his work was always consciously experimental, although the American public was reluctant to accept such work when it aligned closely with European models. Its general aim, then, is to engage if not to offset the perception, as David Savran said of Annette J. Saddik's landmark, *Tennessee Williams and the Theatre of Excess: The Strange, The Crazed, The Queer*, that "Tennessee Williams is the greatest unknown playwright America has produced."[5] What is too often "unknown" is the full, conflicted richness of his creative output and the fact that he was large and contained multitudes.

Chapter 1

T-SHIRT MODERNISM AND PERFORMED MASCULINITIES

THE THEATRICAL REFASHIONINGS OF TENNESSEE WILLIAMS AND WILLIAM INGE

The play cannot be disparaged.

—Arthur Miller of *Streetcar*

In 1947 when Marlon Brando appeared on stage in a torn sweaty T-shirt there was an earthquake.

—Gore Vidal

Something of a dandy drawn to the tuxedo life, the glitz of luxury hotels and room service,[1] Tennessee Williams unleashed a more slovenly, gritty, working-class modernity in his theatrical revolution in which undergarments grew emblematic. Williams's images of postwar masculinity would develop through the work of his protégé, William Inge, continue on the stage and extend into the iconography of film at least through James Dean, Paul Newman, Al Pacino and Sam Shepard as the distinctions between stage and celluloid blurred into performing arts. Such images became dominant in a mode casually called Southern Gothic, generally emblematized by the working man's depression-era uniform, rivetted overalls or "waist overalls." Such anti-fashion began to emerge as high fashion in an evolution from cheap, durable emblems of labor to unisexual, shabby-chic fashion statements by century's end (even as fashion and durability are often at cross purposes), and runways, too, became performative spaces as street style merged with, overlapped and became indistinguishable (price tags excepted) from high style. Once foundational, the mere "under-shirt," the form-fitting, stretch T-shirt, an "unmentionable" at one point, became an emblem, often in tandem with "overalls," or "blue jeans," not only of working-class vitality if not virility but also of rugged, middle-class, heightened (mostly white) masculinity as well. These postwar images extended through the youth rebellion of the 1950s and 1960s, into the subsequent tie dye era of the 1960s and 1970s, the grunge of the 1980s and 1990s, to the general shift in American public appearance from suits to sweats, from neckties to tie dyes, to their eventual co-option by corporate America; that is, the emergence, in what is here called T-Shirt Modernism, of athletic wear and training gear as acceptable, even fashionable, public dress and as emblems of masculine virility. The most immediate beneficiaries of this trend—call it the Kowalski effect, rather, the Williams effect—were at first the principal vendors of male undergarments, Jockey (q.v.) and Hanes, but as trendier, specialized brands like Nike, Reebok, Adidas, Under Armour and Second Skin, or those associated with particular territories and outdoor challenges, like The North Face, High Sierra and Patagonia, emerged, they tended to proclaim adventure, prowess, self-fulfillment, wit and ideologies amid the everyday performance of self while touting their foundational, insular roots with corporate logos emblazoned on every item—and they've crossed gender and class divides. This is fashion (and associated products) for rugged guys and those drawn to them, as humans willingly became corporate shills. Such a tectonic shift in haberdashery, in acceptable public appearance and the recalibration of an exaggerated hypermasculinity owe much to the theatrical revolution unleashed on the Broadway stage by Tennessee Williams (and his collaborators) in December of 1947; Gore Vidal called it "an earthquake."

Born of sexist necessity, the short-sleeved, crew-necked, stretchable, form-fitting, cotton undergarment that formed a "T" when laid out, was at first promoted as an answer to the bachelor's perceived darning ineptitude. Its stretchable cotton replaced the flannel, button-up, usually one-piece, often red "Form Fitting Union Suit," the one-piece, white "long johns" that joined (hence the word Union) top and bottom into a single garment. In Dashiell Hammett's *Maltese Falcon* (1930; film, 1941), for instance, iconic detective Sam Spade, awakened and called to investigate the death of his partner, Miles Archer, dresses in the fashion of his day: "He put on a thin white union-suit, grey socks, black garters, and dark brown shoes" (Chapter 2 "Death in the Fog," 10–11). In F. Scott Fitzgerald's *This Side of Paradise* (1920), on the other hand, the youthful Amory Blaine, a bit more modern and on his way to Princeton, lists his ivy league necessities: "Six suits summer underwear, six suits winter underwear, one sweater or T shirt," both of the latter, that is, pullovers.

In *Auto-da-Fé*, the Tennessee Williams one-act play of 1941—the year that *The Maltese Falcon* was released as a film and six years before the Broadway premiere of *A Streetcar Named Desire*—Mme Duvenet, a rooming house proprietor, offers her sexually repressed, postal employee son, Eloi [El-wah], some life advice, "There are three simple rules I wish you would observe"; the first obtains here as primary, "One: you should wear under-shirts whenever

MEN'S FORM FITTING UNION SUITS.

SIZES: Give breast measure over vest close up under arms, and your height and weight.

A rational garment for men. Try our Union Suits for ease and comfort and you will wonder why you did not wear them before. Our Men's Union or Combination Suits fit. They are carefully and scientifically proportioned. We offer for your consideration only those suits that will fit, and we warrant them to be satisfactory in every particular.

80 Cents for $1.00 Men's Winter Weight Cotton Union Suits.

No. 16R6000 Men's Silver Gray Heavy Cotton Union Suits. Slightly fleeced on the inside, making them very soft and pleasant to the skin. Button down front. A special value at this low price. Finished neck and pearl buttons. Sizes, 34, 36, 38, 40, 42, 44. State breast, height and weight in your order.

Price, per dozen, $9.60; per suit.. ....80c

No. 16R6001 Men's Fine Union Suits, knitted from fine cotton yarn, same quality as the above, but in ecru color. Sizes, breast 34, 36, 38, 40, 42, 44. State height, weight and breast measure in order.

Price, each.............$0.80
Per dozen................ 9.60

If by mail, postage extra, each, 24 cents.

Figure 1.1 Neck-to-ankle Union Suit advertised in the Sears Roebuck catalog for 1902

there's changeable weather" (Williams, 1949, 108). The rule-bound Mme Duvenet does not specify the type of "under-shirt" Eloi should wear, but such a garment suggests a need for insulation and so protection, even in the often oppressive heat of the Vieux Carré district in New Orleans where they reside. His commercial offerings would have been as limited in 1941 as were the possibilities of his sexual expression, but one may have been what was nicknamed, and appropriately so for the repressed Eloi, the "Bachelor Undershirt."

We can readily imagine how scandalized the doting Mme Duvenet would have been were her son to wear such a garment as outerwear, which she would deem *en déshabillé*. She would be as scandalized as she was by Eloi's revelation of the "lewd photograph" that fell from an unsealed envelope he was sorting as a postal employee and that led to a series of climactic and melodramatic events that end with conflagration, self-immolation and, perhaps, rape. The photograph serves as the play's central secret and symbol, especially if one reads Eloi's visit to the youthful sender as a homosexual solicitation, as, apparently, the university student did since he "began to be ugly. Abusive. I can't repeat the charges, the evil suggestions! I ran from the room" (Williams, 1949, 112). The "under-shirt," the "unmentionables" are something of latent material symbols—of repression—suggesting the deeper, conflicted, if not closeted, desire that leads not only to the failed liaison with the university student but also to the melodramatic conflagration, the burning of sexual

Figure 1.2 A 1904 magazine advertisement by Cooper Underwear Company

heretics imbedded in the play's Portuguese title and anticipated by an unseen vendor's *"curiously rich haunting voice"* as something of a tragic choral prelude to Eloi's disclosure and its melodramatic endgame, *"Re-ed Ho-ot, re-ed ho-ot, re-e-e-d!"* (Williams, 1949, 109).

The usual residents of these pre-motel, budget oases for travelers, itinerants and drummers, are described by Williams in "The Strangest Kind of Romance" written about 1946, thus just before *A Streetcar Named Desire*, as "the itinerant, unmarried working men of a nation" (Williams, 1949, 129). Less usual, the boarder at Mme Duvenet's establishment is a woman alone, one Miss Bordelon, the name suspiciously suggesting bordello, to whom Eloi reportedly speaks "so crossly" (Williams, 1949, 103). In another seedy rooming house in the French Quarter, the "Lady of Larkspur Lotion," too, may be a prostitute with Blanche-like fantasies of a Brazilian rubber plantation overlooking, she claims, the Mediterranean and the White Cliffs of Dover! She receives a one-day financial reprieve from writer and fellow boarder, Anton Chekhov (Williams, 1949, 67–72).[2] In the fourth and final "lyrical" scene of "The Strangest Kind of Romance," a T-shirt-wearing former boxer seduces the "Mean—ugly—fat" landlady, Bella Gallaway, or, at least, at the play's finale, "The Boxer slips his arm around her waist. The light is golden, the music is faint and tender." (Williams, 1949, 148). A version of such closing

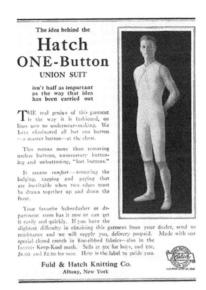

Figure 1.3 Advertisement in the *New Haven Leader*, New Haven, Missouri, October 16, 1919

lines will reemerge at the end of *Streetcar*, written a year later, as the Kowalskis rekindle their erotic relationship after Blanche is committed.[3] That T-shirt-wearing boxer was modeled after one of Williams's "butch" loves (Camille Paglia's term), Pancho Gonzales, or more fully, Amado "Pancho" Rodríguez y González, whom Williams met in Mexico City in 1945 and who, according to Paglia (among others), was one of the models for the "primitive," T-shirt-wearing Stanley Kowalski (Paglia's term, again, 2018, 234).[4]

Such twentieth-century refinements on the constrictive, Victorian-era protective undergarment, especially the introduction of the buttonless "undershirt," grew not only acceptable but also popular as the American military adopted the garment for general issue (hence, G. I.) during World War I. Under certain labor conditions, like a ship's steamy engine rooms or amid hot-climate construction teams, such garments were permissible outerwear, and hence the garment was often associated with perspiration, sweat.[5] With the end of World War II, demobilized G. I.s had grown accustomed to the comfort of so relaxed a dress code, and, moreover, millions of the garments, remainders and, finally, reminders of the war effort, found their way into military surplus stores where they were sold at substantially discounted prices. Such surplus vendors date at least to the Civil War, which was the first American war with a uniform dress code, but their number burgeoned after World War II in proportion to the war's ramped-up industrial output.

Figure 1.4 Wardrobe test for film adaptation of *A Streetcar Named Desire*, August 9, 1950

In 1947, one such demobilized veteran crashed the Broadway stage as Stanley Kowalski in *A Streetcar Named Desire*, a play that would upset Broadway's entertainment expectations, generate not only a theatrical revolution in explicit content in a gritty, contemporary acting style but would also spark a revolution in fashion as well, featuring not only what Camille Paglia calls Kowalski's "blue-denim work clothes" (Paglia, 2018, 233), standard issue working-class garb, but more distinctly, pervasively and originally, his form-fitting undershirts—exposed. No "thin white union-suit" for Mr. Kowalski, as he was part of the G. I. undershirt generation, especially in the climate of the Faubourg Marigny neighborhood of New Orleans in this play that offered "an oppositional strain in American culture that emerged following World War II" (Paglia, 2018, 234). Estimable critic, George Jean Nathan, was wittier and more direct, calling Williams a "Southern Genital-man," and noting further that "the play might have been called The Glans Menagerie" (Nathan cited in Lahr, 2014, 146). *New Yorker* theatre critic and Williams biographer John Lahr continues in summary: "It was the first sighting on the American stage of a sexual male." For Gore Vidal, "In 1947 when Marlon Brando appeared on stage in a torn sweaty T-shirt there was an earthquake." He thought that Kowalski changed the concept of sex in America. Before him, no male was considered erotic. Some were handsomer than others, some had charm. He was essentially a suit, not a body. [...] Marlon played with his cock on stage and that excited people. The mutation was the Williams effect. The male is his obsession, and male sexuality the benchmark. Females are principal characters in his plays because it's through them that you're going to view the male, which is the playwright's objective. (Vidal cited in Lahr, 2014, 146)

Kowalski was a veteran, a Master Sergeant in the Army Engineer Corps in Salerno, the World War II invasion site just south of Naples in the operation to liberate Fascist Italy. Stella introduces her husband, Stanley, to her visiting elder sister, Blanche DuBois, via a photograph and a telling phrase:

> Yes, a different species.
> BLANCHE: In what way? What's he like?
> STELLA: Oh! You can't describe someone you're in love with! Here's a picture of him. (*She hands a photograph to Blanche.*)
> BLANCHE: An officer!
> STELLA: A Master Sergeant in the Engineers' Corps. Those are his decorations" (Williams, 1951, 24).

Those decorations are not detailed, but, several scenes later, Stanley reminds Stella (and thereby the audience) of his military service and thus of his "band of brothers" loyalties: "Mitch is a buddy of mine. We were in the same outfit together—Two-forty-first Engineers. We work in the same plant and now on the same bowling team" (Williams, 1951, 108). Stanley was thus working in the military in what would be T-shirt weather during Operation Avalanche, the invasion of southern Italy in September of 1943. While Stanley was not directly part of an active combat unit, the Axis powers would certainly have targeted whatever the "Two-forty-first Engineers" were building—roads, bridges, airfields, barracks and the like—to slow the allied invasion. He was thus part of what has come to be called "The Greatest Generation," although that's hardly the impression we get of Mr. Kowalski over the course of the play, but the play, and more explicitly the 1951 film, even with the latter's heavy censorship and rewritten, moralistic ending, become something of a fashion show for this "different species" of male and so a different mode of masculinity, and the T-shirt, at times sweat-soaked, at times torn, is its central emblem. It helped that one had a totally buff Marlon Brando filling out those stretch T-s, but Brando, rather Kowalski, in a suit and tie is another sort of image altogether (see Brando's subsequent *Guys and Dolls*, for instance).

Figure 1.5 Marlon Brando as Johnny Strabler in the 1953 American film noir crime film, directed by László Benedek, *The Wild One*

Kowalski is, of course, not only working-class but unabashedly so in all its vitality and virility, what Camille Paglia calls, "the strutting male animal in his sexual prime" (Paglia, 2018, 233), which Stanley flaunts. As he reminds Stella:

> When we first met—you and me—you thought I was common. Well, how right you was. I was common as dirt. You showed me a snapshot of the place with them columns, and I pulled you down off them columns, and how you loved it, having them colored lights going! And wasn't we happy together? Wasn't it all okay till she showed here? […] And wasn't we happy together? Wasn't it all okay? Till she showed here. Hoity-toity, describin' me like an ape.

Stella's response is simply, "Take me to the hospital" (Williams, 1951, 112).

Two years after the film version of *Streetcar*, those crew-necked Tees would be layered, enhanced certainly by another iconic garment, the Schott Perfecto One Star motorcycle jacket (model #618 in black steerhide in 1.2- to 1.4-mm-thick 3-ounce leather) that Brando wore in *The Wild One* (1953) in tandem with his "blue jeans." Such imagery, Paglia notes, "prefigured the youth rebellion of the 1950s--including rock and roll to whose iconography Brando would contribute" (Paglia, 2018, 234). The snakeskin jacket Brando's Val Xavier wore in *The Fugitive Kind*, the 1960 film remake of Williams's *Orpheus Descending*, which ran for only 68 performances on Broadway in 1957, might have become as iconic, but Val's jacket was unique, not commercially replicable. The Schott

Perfecto over a white T-shirt, on the other hand, became the uniform of a generation, especially for those with a contrarian spirit, rebels, often, without a cause. *Orpheus* itself was a rewriting of Williams's first produced play, *Battle of Angels*, from which the line "the fugitive kind" derives, but *Battle of Angels* closed in its Boston preview within two weeks of its December 1940 opening. The Boston Police Commissioner called it "a play about cheap, white trash [...] Indecent and improper [...] Lascivious and immoral"; another councilman called it "putrid."

> For the play to continue in Boston, censors demanded certain lines be cut, including: "All references to [the] deity and Christ," and "to [the] stigmatae" on the hero's hands. A painting of the hero which resembled Jesus started a scandal of its own among those in the audience who hadn't been following the plot and thought a portrait of their Savior was being desecrated. A temporary solution had been to put the painting in a closet. Eventually the painting was changed so it looked nothing like Jesus. Then it could be destroyed in Boston without offense. (*Battle of Angels*)

The title has its origins in an even earlier effort of 1937, a one-act play of that title set in a Depression-era flophouse that betrays its debt to Clifford Odets, and it might have resonated with the Eugene O'Neill of *Hughie*, O'Neill's one-acter, set in 1928, but *Hughie* was written only in 1941 and not performed until 1958, and then in Sweden. And *Orpheus* was originally titled *Something Wild in the Country* and produced under that title in its Washington, DC, and Philadelphia tryouts; it was also the working title for *Battle of Angels* before its Boston tryout. But the root of this strutting new masculinity was the stretch T-shirt that defined a generation's sense of "cool" as depicted in the 1950 Warner Bros. wardrobe photo in anticipation of the filming of *A Streetcar Named Desire*. The contrast is sharp with the attire for Karl Malden's Mitch—a product of the same "Two-forty-first Engineers"—who appears in jacket and tie (since he's courting Blanche) and so looks like he stepped out of (or into) *The Maltese Falcon*. Visually, then, contrasting images of prewar and postwar masculinity appear in a single shot. And even the famous 1948 illustration of the "Poker Night" (an early working title for the play) scene of *Streetcar* by Thomas Hart Benton, used as the cover image to the first Signet, mass market paperback edition of the play, foregrounded undergarments: a seductive Blanche in semi-transparent negligee but featuring a drunken and enraged, muscular Stanley leaning over the poker table in his sleeveless white T-shirt.[6] Blanche's sexuality is further foregrounded when the Benton painting is cropped in the Penguin edition of the *A Streetcar Named Desire and other Plays* (2000). The image of an exhibitionist Blanche is enlarged to accentuate her breasts and protruding nipples, as the more modest, demure Stella covers and so shields herself.[7]

Despite its provocative cover, this 2000 reprint in the Penguin Classics series astonishingly still uses the censored version of Blanche's story of her husband's, Allan Grey's homosexuality (183), the same version of the text used in its 1962 edition (183), the cover photo for which showed an image from the 1949 London Aldwych Theatre production with Vivien Leigh and American-born actor Bonar Colleano (further production details in Chapter 2).

Brando's image from *The Wild One* was further iconized in the silkscreen on linen Warhol portraits of Brando on his Triumph 650cc 6T Thunderbird motorcycle, particularly those multiples that highlight the reproducibility of the image, the Brando diptych and "Four Marlons" in particular, that are themselves now widely reproduced commercially on T-shirts. But Warhol's Brando images, like his Monroe and Presley depictions, were already nostalgic by 1966, and so Warhol's silkscreen innovations were not only gestures of recuperation of a lost era and spirit, replaced by other images of masculinity and sexuality, but Warhol paved the way for the commercial profusion of such nostalgic images. After Warhol, hypermasculinity and hyperfemininity were up for sale.

Williams was not the first American playwright to feature working-class vitality and sweaty masculinity on the Broadway stage, of course. Eugene O'Neill had featured rugged stevedores and sailors in his earliest theatrical efforts. He was associated in the first decade of the twentieth century with politically leftist groups in New York's bohemian enclave of Greenwich Village and their summer retreat in Provincetown, Massachusetts, where his first production, *Bound East for Cardiff*, was read and performed by the newly formed Provincetown Players at their Playhouse in the summer of 1916, with a subsequent transfer to the group's recently converted Greenwich Village Theater at 139 MacDougal Street (the old address) that fall. O'Neill would premiere some 15 plays with the Provincetown Players before 1922. *Beyond the Horizon* opened on Broadway in 1920 and subsequently won O'Neill his first Pulitzer Prize. Labor itself was on full, charismatic display in the expressionistically inflected *The Hairy Ape* that premiered at the Provincetown Playhouse in 1922 and moved to the Provincetown Theatre on MacDougal Street in March of that year for 108 performances: "That preposterous little theater has one of the most cramped stages that New York has ever known" (Woollcott cited in Brantley, 2001, 63). Although Yank is referred to as "a filthy beast" by steel heiress Mildred Douglas as part of O'Neill's anti-industrial screed, the play was "doubtless headed for Broadway," according to reviewer Alexander Woollcott, who called it "vital and interesting and teeming with life"

Figure 1.6 Tempera and oil on linen painting of one of the play's iconic scenes by American regionalist painter, Thomas Hart Benton. *Poker Night* (1948) now in the Whitney Museum's permanent collection

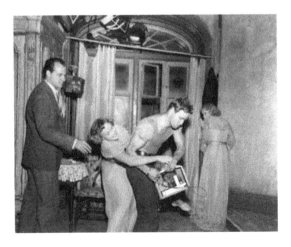

Figure 1.7 Scene from the 1951 film version of *A Streetcar Named Desire* demonstrating sharply contrasting modes of dress between Mitch (left) and Stanley (center)

(Woollcott cited in Brantley 2001, 62–63). Yank is strong and hardworking, but, without a social or cultural identity, this image of robust masculinity reverts to being "a hairy ape," suggesting something of a degeneration of the species at a time when the "idealization of lower-class masculinity was rampant," as James A. Robinson phrases it (Robinson, 1995, 98). Robinson would go on to discuss the "hairy ape" in terms of the "masculine primitive," part of "the *fin de siècle*'s vigorous reassertion of masculinity" in response to a first wave of feminism (Robinson, 98). Williams, in turn, will have Kowalski invoke Louisiana's populist governor, "What do you think you are? A pair of queens. Remember what Huey Long said—'Every Man is a King!' And I am the king around here, so don't forget it!" (Williams 1951, 107).

O'Neill's recalibrations of Greek myth, however, would finally have the more lasting impact on a still-emerging, serious, American theater than his foregrounding of the "masculine primitive." *Desire under the Elms*, a reworking of Euripides's play *Hippolytus*, O'Neill's Eben, Abbie and Ephraim corresponding, roughly, to Hippolytus, Phaedra and Theseus, features passion and desire in the tradition of Greek tragedy; it was produced by Provincetown Players off-Broadway in 1924, playing an additional nine months after its move uptown to Broadway. Its revival in 1952, directed by Harold Clurman, was part of the American National Theater and Academy (ANTA), the attempt to establish an American national theater as an alternative to Broadway commercialism (i.e., as a theater for the whole nation in conjunction with the Federal Theater Project),[8] anticipated the 1958 film version with its serious miscasting of Sophia Loren as Abbie. O'Neill may have explored and reflected certain currents of American masculinity, but he would not redefine it as Williams would.

Clifford Odets's *Waiting for Lefty* (1935) was also part of such rampant "idealization of lower class masculinity"; it was staged by what Paglia calls "the leftist ensemble-oriented Group Theater" (Paglia, 2018, 234), founded by Harold Clurman, Lee Stasburg and Cheryl Crawford, in January of 1935. The play was in keeping with the "Living Newspaper" theatrical experiments, the format developed by the Federal Theater Project (disbanded in 1939). It was first published in *New Theatre* magazine with the subtitle "A Play in Six Scenes, Based on the New York City Taxi Strike of February 1934." Real-life striker, Samuel Orner, noted that Odets based the meeting scene on a real meeting in the Bronx where Orner addressed his fellow cabbies: "He must have taken notes because so many lines in *Waiting for Lefty* were the same as in the meeting, almost word for word."[9] As such it was close to the work being done by Elmer Rice, one of the forces in the short-lived "Living Newspaper" theatrical experiments, his own *The Adding Machine* of 1923 and *Street Scene*, which began as 15 scenes of life in New York and which won the Pulitzer Prize in 1929, paving the way. And Rice would have his influence on

Williams. In what is often referred to as one of Williams's "apprentice plays," *Stairs to the Roof*, completed in 1941 and subtitled *A Prayer for the Wild of Heart That Are Kept in Cages*,[10] details the dehumanizing effects of repeated, robotic office work that constitutes the cage, like that in which Williams worked for International Shoes in St. Louis, Missouri; this utopian fantasy of escape is dedicated to "all the little wage earners of the world." The protagonists in *Stairs to the Roof*, like those of *The Adding Machine*, moreover, tend to be less-developed characters than representative abstractions. Rice's male lead, one "Mr. Zero," for instance, bears a certain resonance with Williams's female lead called simply "Girl"; Rice has Messrs. One, Two, Three, etc.; Williams has Messrs. P, D, Q, T. And Williams's *Camino Real* of 1953 began life as the episodic and fantasy-driven *Ten Blocks on the Camino Real*. Directed by Elia Kazan at the Actors Studio in 1949, *Ten Blocks*, or scenes, may owe something to Rice's episodic *Street Scene*, especially in Kazan's attempt to refashion it into naturalistic theater.[11]

But the roaring twenties also featured groundbreaking, politically charged work like the proto-feminist, expressionist-inflected *Machinal* (1928), subtitled "A Tragedy in 10 Episodes," from Sophie Treadwell, with its focus on a loveless marriage motivated by economic necessity. Passion for another man drives the protagonist, Ruth Snyder, to murder her husband, but even with such a libidinal theme the play was not infused with the sort of raw sexuality that emerged with Stanley Kowalski in 1947.[12] Writing in the *New York Times*, Brooks Atkinson would praise *Machinal* as "Fraught with a beauty unfamiliar to the stage. [...] the tragedy of one who lacks strength; she is not adaptable; she submits. [...] Being the exposition of a character, stark and austere in style, *Machinal* makes no excuses for the tragedy it unfolds" (Atkinson, 2001, 18). Even featuring Clark Gable as "Man (Young Woman's lover)" in his Broadway debut and based on the sensational and much publicized Snyder-Gray murder case,[13] *Machinal* ran for only 95 performances on Broadway and has rarely been revived.[14] What it lacked, like *Street Scene*, say, or failed to stage, may be such T-shirt modernism described most acutely by Blanche DuBois. To Stella's "I wish you'd stop taking it for granted that I'm in something I want to get out of Blanche DuBois" after she had been abused by Stanley the night before and left, at least until the famous "Stella!" scene, Blanche returns to the "hairy ape" or the "masculine primitive" theme, "[...] you're not old. You can get out" (Williams, 1951, 65) and adds:

What you are talking about is desire—just brutal Desire. The name of that rattle-trap streetcar that bangs through the Quarter, up one old narrow street and down another. [...] May I speak plainly? [...] If you'll forgive me, he's common [...] He's like an animal. He has an animal's habits. There's even something subhuman about him. Thousands of years have passed him right by, and there he is. Stanley Kowalski, survivor of the Stone Age, bearing the raw meat home from the kill in the jungle. And you—you here waiting for him. Maybe he'll strike you or maybe grunt and kiss you, that's if kisses have been discovered yet. Night falls and the other apes gather. [...] His poker night you call it. This party of apes! Somebody growls—somebody snatches at something—the fight is on! *God*! Maybe we are a long way from being made in God's image, but Stella—my sister—there has been *some* progress since then! [...] In some kinds of people some tender feelings have had some little beginning! [...] *Don't—don't hang back with the brutes*! (Williams, 1951, 71–72)

Stella's critique of Stanley's atavistic or stunted libido takes on considerable irony when her own backstory of less than discriminant, compensatory sex at the Hotel Flamingo in the fictional Laurel, Mississippi, where Blanche repairs after having lost the family manse, Belle Reve, is brought to light by Stanley, a backstory that Blanche has herself carefully deflected. Blanche's sexual encounters with her high school students, furthermore, could be considered criminal, statutory rape, depending on the ages of those students and the laws of the day, to which group, as a reflection of Allan Grey, perhaps, she remains compulsively drawn even while living with the Kowalskis. As Blanche tells an adolescent, whom she calls "Young, young, young man!," collecting subscriptions for the *Evening Star* newspaper at the end of Scene Five, "You make my mouth water [*She touches his cheek lightly and smiles* (...)]" as she confesses her *desire* to "kiss you [...] softly and sweetly on your mouth!" The scene depicts what Blanche had earlier denigrated as "just brutal desire," but it was left on the cutting room floor of the film as was the overt admission of her predilection for young boys, "I've got to be good—and keep my hands off children" (Williams, 1951, 84), a scene that returns us to her sexual disgrace in Laurel, Mississippi. By today's standard she would have to register as a sex offender and register as such wherever she traveled, if she were allowed to travel beyond the jurisdiction of the State of Mississippi, that is, where her crimes, and that is the word, were committed. At the very least she was (or is) a sexual predator, which modulates our understanding of her characterization of Stanley and her advice to Stella above, and as such she is part of the familial "epic fornications" that she alludes to and to which she attributes the loss of their ancestral home:

Belle Reve as, piece by piece, our improvident grandfathers and fathers and uncles and brothers exchanged the land for their epic fornications— to put it plainly! [...] The four letter word deprived us of our plantation, till finally all that was left—and Stella can verify that—was the house itself. (Williams, 1951, 43)

In *Streetcar* such "epic fornications" and sexual predation are, thus, transgenerational and ungendered. The film version of 1951 would expunge not only references to homosexuality but also much of the overt sexuality (and so the work's sexual energy) as well, reducing the final rape scene to an ambiguous sexual encounter, the violence of which Williams fought to restore, to no avail:

> The rape of Blanche by Stanley is a pivotal, integral truth in the play, without which the play loses its meaning which is the ravishment of the tender, the sensitive, the delicate by the savage and brutal forces of modern society. It is a poetic plea for comprehension. I did not beg the issue by making Blanche a totally 'good' person, and Stanley a totally "bad." (Williams, 2007, 355)

Blanche's not being "a totally 'good' person" is, in part, the result of her inability to "keep my hands off children," and Blanche is among those included in *A Prayer for the Wild of Heart That Are Kept in Cages*; but then, so is Stanley, even as Williams sees his "amplitude of amorous tools [... as] less attractive" (Grissom, 2013).

According to Jeffrey B. Loomis, in fact, Williams was conflicted not only about the play's central sexual tensions but also about the mood or tone of those tensions as well. Like most of Williams's work, his central idea or situation for *Streetcar* went through not only a series of drafts but also through various versions, with ideas often tested or expressed in different and conflicting genres. Loomis calls such tensions "Dialogues of Dueling Genres": "Williams's ongoing personal dialogue between comic and quasi-tragic genres [...] manifested itself in the progressive development of *A Streetcar Named Desire*. In crafting that play, he repeatedly produced manuscripts looking like ragtag stitching together of wildly opposed plots. [...] [A]lmost all the drafts, whenever they each were written, eccentrically mesh together different genre approaches" (Loomis, 165). Most apposite to our discussion is the nature of Blanche's sexual relationship with her brother-in-law. In the version called "Interior: Panic" (University of Texas archive 44.3),[15] Loomis notes that "Like Stanley in the 1947 text, Jack robustly reports to his pal George that Blanche/Gladys has been prodigiously promiscuous (behavior to which that woman freely admits within this particular tragicomic collection of scenes)" (Loomis, 2017, 166). Williams's "representation of inner struggle and undeniable sexual urge is highly mixed in tone, as evidenced in the pre-*Streetcar* draft set in Atlanta titled 'The Primary Colors' (Texas 44.10/1)"; Loomis continues, "The personage known as Blanche sexually leers at her brother-in-law Ralph. [...] Eventually, though, a long, culminating scene of her [Blanche] and Howdy [Mitch] sharing large amounts of booze leads them finally into the bedroom for sex. Enjoying themselves in spates of rollicking laughter, they startle Ralph [Stanley] and Stella from offstage" (Loomis, 166). In the draft called "The Passion of the Moth" (Texas 44.8), "Blanche and Stanley are revealed exulting in the aftershock of their rousing previous night's supposedly consensual sexual congress. [...] while Stella was bearing a baby in the maternity ward of the maternity hospital, her sister Blanche was having the best sex of her life with her highly satisfied brother-in-law Stanley. Afterward she proclaims that she will leave her sister's home, to become a professional 'lady of the evening'" (Loomis, 166, see also Staggs, 1–8). While Williams struggled through a series of sexual possibilities and generic structures in his drafts, his final take leaves little ambiguity in the final scene that is not an instance of consensual sex, or even of sex per se since rape is fundamentally an act of violence.

The earlier sensation of this period featuring non-normative sexuality was, however, the stage adaptation of Erskine Caldwell's 1932 novel, *Tobacco Road*, which brought share croppers and southern Gothic grotesquery to Broadway. The novel was adapted to the stage by Jack Kirkland, and this story of Depression-era southern poverty, squalor and curious early marriages (including the purchase of an underaged bride for $5) and including "one of the grossest episodes ever put on the stage" (Atkinson, 2001, 85), ran on Broadway for a stunning 3,182 performances over a period of eight years. It was followed by a film version with its much-altered story line, directed by John Ford in 1941. In comparison, *A Streetcar Named Desire*, itself a smash hit, played for 855 performances between December of 1947 and December of 1949. While the stage adaptation of *Tobacco Road* is "still Erskine Caldwell's novel at heart," as Brooks Atkinson noted of the play (Atkinson, 2001, 85–86), Bosley Crowther opened his *New York Times* review of the film with a disclaimer:

> Right off, the answer is no—and you who have entertained doubts that the screen version of "Tobacco Road," which John Ford has made for Twentieth Century-Fox, might somewhat resemble the stage play may rest assured that it does not. As a matter of fact, it barely resembles a believable slice of life, and just comes under the wire as an amusing but pointless film. (Crowther, 1941)

While the novel and stage adaptation depict something like depraved base instincts, physical deformities and mental deficiencies of the southern poor, which had the character of sensational pulp fiction and included the visual imagery of the working, farming class in overalls but without much redeeming beauty or dignity, it lacked the sort of "brutal desire" that Blanche describes. It was banned in the United Kingdom for a time and in a number of major American cities for its perceived immoralities, but Atkinson admitted that

> the theatre has never sheltered a fouler or more degenerate parcel of folks than the hardscrabble family of Lester. [...] It is the blunt truth of the characters he is describing, and it leaves a malevolent glow of poetry [...]. As Jeeter Lester, Henry Hull gives the performance of his career. Plays as clumsy and rudderless as "Tobacco Road" seldom include so many scattered items that leave such a vivid impression. (Atkinson, 2001, 85–86)

Even more sensational was Caldwell's 1933 follow-up novel, *God's Little Acre*, which sold some 10 million copies, but which appeared while *Tobacco Road* was still running on Broadway. The 1958 film version would take advantage of the waning influence of the Hays Commission and so would come closer to the mark, but by 1958 Williams (and Kowalski) had already defined the terrain. *Cat on a Hot Tin Roof* had opened in 1955 and won the Pulitzer Prize for that year. (The award was controversial, however, since the Pulitzer committee's choice seems to have been Clifford Odets's *The Flowering Peach*, which decision was overruled by Joseph Pulitzer.) The film version, with Elizabeth Taylor and Paul Newman replacing Barbara Bel Geddes and Ben Gazzara of the Elia Kazan-directed Broadway production, sanitized of its overt homosexual references, appeared in 1958. *Suddenly, Last Summer* (part of a twin bill with *Something Unspoken* as an evening called *Garden District*) opened off-Broadway in January of 1958 as well, and *Sweet Bird of Youth* (which developed from *The Pink Bedroom* of 1956) opened on Broadway in 1959, starring Paul Newman and Geraldine Page and directed by Kazan. While Williams's works endure as the high-water mark of American theater, Caldwell languishes as contemporary assessments have been less than kind to him, finally treating his work as clichéd pulp fiction. Dan B. Miller noted in his 1995 biography, *Erskine Caldwell: The Journey from Tobacco Road*, that Caldwell offered "a rebuke to the perfumed 'moonlight and magnolias' literature of the south. Yet," as Dwight Garner observes, finally, "it's almost impossible not to read the most ludicrously grim passages of *Tobacco Road* as very black humor" (Miller cited in Garner, 2006). Writing in *Slate*, Garner goes on to suggest that, despite "the blinkered cultural stereotypes Caldwell locked into cement [... the appeal of the work had] everything to do with the fact that few novels have as much stripped-down force and inspire as much terror and pity. The force comes from that fact that Caldwell's id—his naked obsessions with sex, class, and violence—cuts the surface of every page like a dorsal fin" (Garner, 2006).

But Caldwell's "naked obsessions with sex, class, and violence" differ fundamentally from the rawness of desire and libidinous energy with which Williams infuses *Streetcar*, which was never without its lyricism, poetic imagery, beauty in language and visual appeal. That Williams line of libidinous energy might find its parallel in Faulkner, at least the Faulkner of *Sanctuary* (1931, film 1961), an anticipation of *Tobacco Road*, perhaps, or its Temple Drake sequel, *Requiem for a Nun*,[16] a novel written in three acts, which was thus easily adapted to the stage. *Requiem* opened on Broadway in 1959, but its major successes were in Europe where it was embraced by such figures as Albert Camus, who translated it into French in 1956, and Erwin Piscator, who staged it at the Schiller Theater in 1955 (Izard and Hieronymus, 1970). That libidinous drive would continue with a playwright who in many respects was a Williams protégé, William Inge. In his *New York Times* tribute to Inge on his death, Williams recounts their first meeting:

> I met Bill Inge in December, 1944, when I returned home briefly to St. Louis. At that time, he was writing for the *Star-Times*, doing dramatic criticism and interviews and, I think, also serving as music critic.

> This was during the Chicago break-in [try out] of *The Glass Menagerie* and Bill came to our suburban home to interview me. He was embarrassingly "impressed" by my burgeoning career as a playwright. It's always lonely at home now: my friends have all dispersed. I mentioned this to Bill and he cordially invited me to his apartment near the river. We had a gala night among his friends. Later we attended the St. Louis Symphony together. He made my homecoming an exceptional pleasure.

> When I returned to *Menagerie* in Chicago, Bill shortly arrived to "attend and cover" the play, and I believe he was sincerely overwhelmed by the play and the fabulous Laurette Taylor, giving her last and greatest performance. A year or two later, I was back in St. Louis and we met again. He had now retired as journalist and was teaching English at Washington University, not far from our home, and was living in the sort of neo-Victorian white frame house that must have reminded him of his

native Kansas. There, one evening, he shyly produced a play that he had written, *Come Back, Little Sheba*. He read it to me in his beautifully quiet, and expressive voice: I was deeply moved by the play and I immediately wired Audrey Wood[17] about it and urged him to submit it to her. She was equally impressed and Bill became her client almost at once. (Williams, 1973, 1)

And Inge would credit Williams as inspiration as he wrote in his diary: "Tennessee had shown me the dynamic example of the connection between art and life [...] I had never known where to look for material. [...] Now I knew where to look for a play—inside myself" (Lahr, 2014, 406). Williams and Inge also shared a director to whom each was devoted, another product of the Actors Studio, Elia Kazan, but over whose attention they would compete. Inge wanted Kazan to direct *Picnic*,[18] and Kazan was torn between the Inge play and Williams's first "experimental" play: "Kazan thought about doing the [Inge] play, but he felt duty bound to work with Tenn on *Camino Real*, an experimental play he had fathered, encouraged, taught to walk." That is, Kazan had staged a one-act version in 10 scenes or "Ten Blocks on the Camino Real" at the Actors Studio in 1949.[19] "Tenn was being told that he was playing it safe," Kazan said.

He needed to break out of his safe and successful stride and do something new. I liked *Picnic*, and I thought I could do something with it, but I went to the dance that Tenn had created, but I feel I had a relationship with Inge and with *Picnic*. I asked him, as I often do with playwrights, "Which of these characters is Bill Inge?" and without hesitation he told me that they all had pieces of Bill Inge, but more than any others, he was Helen, the older neighbor who harvests good will and cakes, but who is more shaken by the beauty of Hal, the wandering phallus. "How is that you?" I asked. "She is the witness," Bill told me, "and all of my life is on the side, watching, waiting, witnessing." (Grissom, 2013)

Kazan had told Williams after *Sweet Bird of Youth* "that he [Kazan] would direct anything that he [Williams] wrote 'sight unseen'" (Lahr, 2014, 406), but such loyalty had its limits. On April 21, 1960, Kazan withdrew from directing the Williams comedy, *A Period of Adjustment*, in order to direct the film version of Inge's *Splendor in the Grass*, to whom he now felt a greater loyalty because "I had initiated the project. I made him write it" (Lahr, 2014, 406–7); that is, Kazan had fashioned a film script from Inge's prose treatment of the story and for which, as it turned out, Inge won the Academy Award for Best Film Script.

As Lahr says, "That ended the most important theatrical collaborations of twentieth-century American theater" (Lahr, 2014, 405–6). It didn't help that "Williams was openly jealous, even sometimes bitchy about Inge who had three hits in a row, including *Bust Stop* and *Picnic*" (Lahr, 2014, 406). *Picnic* would win the Pulitzer Prize for drama in 1953, among other awards.

For his part Williams was a keen critic of Inge's version of this new, modernist masculinity because they shared a vision, a queering of masculinity in their hyperbolic images of the masculine amid a repressed age:

> "That sad salesman is eroticized by virtue of his proximity to Hal, who can and does arouse everyone," Tenn said. "Hal reminds everyone of either a past and great carnal encounter, or one that was dreamed of. Bill and I first knew the joys of men through pornography, then dangerous viewings at gyms and locker rooms. That is when we learned the power of male attraction. I poured all of this memory and longing into Stanley [Kowalski] and asked that it be understood that these were men who pushed otherwise sane and sensible women into dire and mendacious circumstances. Bill gave us Hal, a man who traveled, leaving a trail of desire and frustration. I didn't show the effect of Stanley on anyone but Blanche, but Bill shows us what a man, a man almost mythic in sexual power, can do to a community, male and female, and, we gather, predominantly heterosexual." (Grissom, 2013)

Williams would try his hand at such "a wandering phallus" with the much reworked script that became the film, *The Fugitive Kind* (1960).

Williams's comparisons of Hal and Stanley are especially astute:

> "There is a power that comes from physical beauty, from sexual superiority," Tenn told me. "Few things are as arousing as those who possess an amplitude of amorous tools and can understand the kismet of placement. It is terribly, terribly charming and addictive. What is more menacing—and far less attractive—is the knowing of some of just how lucky and glorious they are. That would be Stanley: He knows you're looking at and wanting what the gods have hung from him [at least this is Stanley's perception of how Blanche sees him]. I don't think this of Hal: I think Hal is befuddled by everything, unlucky in everything. I think the love he feels for Madge unsettles and surprises him; it's not another fuck on the tuck-and-roll seat at the local drive in. This is real. Hal knows he's trash, but he wants a redeemer, and women love to redeem their men [cf. Blanche and Allen, perhaps], and both Madge and Rosemary

will redeem their men, make them better. No one on earth can or will change Stanley; he feels infallible and will swing an arm or his cock at any impediment that may arise. Hal wants someone to calm and clean him; pour some unguent on the wounds—physical and psychic—that litter the Grecian form." (Grissom, 2013)

But Inge's staying power was considerably less—and his late work denigrated more sharply—than that of Williams. Reviewing the papers of Inge's platonic love relationship with actress Barbara Baley, Diana Bertolini notes: "Though extremely popular and highly regarded in his heyday, Inge went into a sharp decline following a devastating article written by critic Robert Brustein in *Harper's Magazine* in November of 1958 ['The men-taming women of William Inge,' q.v.], on the occasion of the opening of *The Dark at the Top of the Stairs*. Brustein accused Inge of 'mediocrity' and manipulation:'Inge can maintain his affirmations only by a simplistic view of life and a careful selection of characters.' The article was less a review of the play than an attack on Inge's entire *oeuvre* and so on his success, the essay described as a 'critical mugging'" (Bertolini, 2013). On the other hand, "Robert Brustein perceives Stanley as the [D. H.] Lawrence hero 'whose sexuality, though violent, is unmental, unspiritual, and, therefore, in some way free from taint'" (Bloom, 1988, 19).

The lives of both playwrights were, unfortunately, cut short, that of Williams the result of an almost inexplicable accident, that of Inge by his own hand. In his 1971 *New York Times* obituary of Inge, Paul L. Montgomery wrote:

In the summer of 1950, Mr. Inge began work on another play. He decided it should take place 'in the sunshine' in his native Kansas, a recollection of the murmur of women talking on a front porch on a summer evening. He set up what he called 'a little fortress of women,' and then had it breached by a brawny wastrel just arrived in town [, Hal].

The play was "Picnic," starring Ralph Meeker, Janice Rule and two newcomers named Kim Stanley and Paul Newman. It was the hit of the 1953 season, and rights were sold to the movies for $300,000. (Montgomery, 1973)

Newman would be the next iteration of Williams's brand of T-shirt modernism as he took over the role of Hal in *Picnic* but was replaced by the then better known William Holden for the film version. He would come to the fore as another vagabond, Ben Quick, in *The Long Hot Summer* (1958)—story by fellow southern writer William Faulkner, the film script based in part on Faulkner's "The Hound" published in *Harper's* in August of 1931 (152–64) and subtitled, "A Dramatic Book from the Four-Book Novel, *The Hamlet*" (the definite article disambiguating it from a famous play similarly titled), Faulkner's *Snopes* "tetralogy." The Signet "Dramatic Book" was as a cheap paperback issued to follow up on the success of the film and included both an announcement of Faulkner's Nobel Prize and the supermarket teaser, "Primitive Passion."[20] That "power of male attraction" that Williams and Inge celebrated (but Caldwell missed) would find its replications in the rebellious spirit of James Dean in his (only) three films—*East of Eden* (directed by Elia Kazan, 1953), the iconic *Rebel without a Cause* (1955) and *Giant* (1956)—that continued in Newman's films like *The Hustler* (1961), *Hud* (1963) and *Cool Hand Luke* (1967), and it appears even as late as in the work of Al Pacino, although T-shirt modernism was passé by the Pacino era having, by then, gone through the tie-dye fads of the 1960s and 1970s, the grunge of the 1980s, and the contemporary human billboard qualities of overt corporate logos, restaurant promotion, political slogans, religious homilies and, particularly, sports team affiliations of its current phase. The 2006 film reissue of *Streetcar Named Desire* includes Brando's 1947 screen test for a movie that would be called *Rebel without a Cause*, but differed from the 1955 novel.[21] That test was conducted before Brando's explosion on Broadway as Stanley Kowalski on December 3, 1947, and the 1951 film adaptation of *A Streetcar Named Desire* subsequently made Brando an international celebrity well before the inarticulations of his Johnny Strabler in *The Wild One* (1953).

Its peak may have come when Hollywood functioned as Broadway west. Despite the sanitizing effects of the Hays Commission (1934–54 or so when its influence began to wane), the national morality imposed by Postmaster General Will Hays (known popularly as the Hays Code or the Motion Picture Production Code),[22] advertising for works featuring T-shirt Modernism bordered on the salacious. Such imagery was most often associated with hot weather settings like the American South and Southwest; for Williams, by the 1960s, such imagery finally began to feel like reruns, like something of a creative rut, even as the images he unleashed took on a cultural life of their own in the recalibration of performing selves. Williams struggled to move away from or beyond those expectations into more self-referential, experimental works like *Out Cry* or *The Two-Character Play* and the biographical study of Zelda Fitzgerald in *Clothes for a Summer Hotel*, withholding from audiences the theatrical and filmic images he had developed and they had come to expect. Such imagery would resonate afresh for a time in the work of Sam Shepard. As both playwright and actor on stage and in film, he capitalized on such T-shirt Modernism for works set in the sparsely populated deserts of the Southwest with characters whose inarticulation rivaled that of Stanley Kowalski. On coming to New York in the heady 1960s, Shepard achieved theatrical success almost instantly:

> In New York he quickly found an interest in writing, which brought him to the emerging world of avant-garde theater on the Lower East Side. A succession of award-winning plays followed: *Chicago, Icarus's Mother, Red Cross, La Turista,* and *Forensic and the Navigators* all won Obie Awards in the off- and off-off-Broadway categories between 1965 and 1968. During this time he was also aided by grants from the Rockefeller and Guggenheim foundations. (Howe, 1997)

His *Buried Child* would win the Pulitzer Prize in 1979, and he was a nominated finalist for two others: *True West* in 1983 and *Fool for Love* in 1984.[23] But for a time—the period of Williams's greatest triumphs, at least—the images that he generated in 1947 would define an age and a gender. By the 1960s, however, they came to be considered nostalgic as the sexual and aesthetic taboos against which they played began to collapse. Censorship eased and theater itself began to change course, to merge with various hybridizations, into the mixed media of performance art, and to overlap other, broader forms of performance like fashion shows and music videos.[24] Those T-shirt images remained strong, however, in the parallel, post–World War II cheap paperback phenomenon as companies like Signet Books, an offshoot of Penguin and a subsidiary of New American Library,[25] and Pan Books in the United Kingdom moved literature, even classic literature, across class divides to a mass audience by selling their less durable commodities not through stuffy or intimidating bookstores but through railway station kiosks, pharmacies, supermarkets, convenience stores and the like. Their arresting cover images could be found beside the checkout counter to tempt the impulse buyer, often featuring figures *en déshabillé.* The almost technical, rarefied experimentalism of William Faulkner could, thus, be found alongside sensationalist journals and bodice rippers, their covers belying qualitative differences. Such film advertising and the paperback revolution would pave the way for the court case that finally would end formal, overt literary censorship in the United States with the publication of the unexpurgated *Lady Chatterley's Lover* by Grove Press in 1959 (jointly with Reader's Subscription in the United States and subsequently with Penguin Books in the United Kingdom a year later). Williams himself would struggle with such cultural shifts as his medium, theater, too, changed around him, passed him by, even, as he struggled to catch up and to "stop playing it safe," as Kazan suggested, but as lasting as any individual work he produced was the legacy of those iconic images of modern males in T-shirts that defined an era and whose echoes, corrupted and commodified as they have become, persist. The cultural thread traced here developed far beyond stage or film imagery, beyond the work of costume designers or a single director or playwright, but its impetus is generated by a post-World War II spirit epitomized by the crowing performative, if not exhibitionist, masculinity of one Stanley Kowalski.

Chapter 2

"INTENSE HONESTY": RACE, SEX AND CROSS-CULTURAL PERSPECTIVES

For the first time in its history, English theatre has been swayed and shaped by America.

—Kenneth Tynan, 1948

Reviewing a series of productions for the *New York Times* on December 15, 1988, under the title, "In London: Taking Williams Seriously," Frank Rich makes an insightful comment about America's most influential playwright five years after his freakish, accidental death in 1983:

> In death Tennessee Williams is more often regarded by the American theater as a tragic icon than as a playwright worthy of further artistic investigation. The reverse is true in London, where the Williams canon, neglected by the major companies during the writer's lifetime, is suddenly being rediscovered. (Rich, Section C, p. 15)

Rich's observation could be extended to the better part of Europe, of course, where the most serious rediscoveries of Williams's work seem centered. Much of the neglect of Williams in the United States has indeed been fueled by preoccupations with the playwright's biography, his tempestuous life and sensational, even clownish public and media appearances, all of which often overshadowed his art. His *Memoirs* in particular, published in 1975 and admittedly written for the cash advance, was exceptionally candid about his sexuality and love life and so did little to redeem his falling reputation. On the other side of the Atlantic, Williams's early plays were quickly performed by allies and in newly liberated European countries, including the European premiere of *The Glass Menagerie* in Stockholm in 1946 (although Sweden was nominally neutral during World War II) then in London in 1948; *A Streetcar Named Desire* opened in most major European capitals, including Rome, London and Paris, by 1949.[1] These were subsequently followed by "the critically controversial yet financially successful Paris production of *Cat on a Hot Tin Roof* a decade later" (Gindt, 2013, 19). In a Britain still struggling to emerge from its Victorian legacy, Williams's more sexually charged work often appeared in heavily censored productions, and early publications tended to follow those sanitized versions of his work. The two 1980s London revivals under discussion in Rich's review include *Cat on a Hot Tin Roof*, which opened on Broadway in March of 1955 under the direction of Elia Kazan, but saw its full, uncensored public British premier at London's National Theatre only in this 1988 production under the "sizzling direction" of Howard Davies, with Lindsay Duncan and Ian Charleson (the production revived on Broadway in March 1990 with American actors Kathleen Turner, Daniel Hugh Kelly and Charles Durning). The second offering is Peter Hall's inaugural production for the Peter Hall Company, the group he formed upon retiring from his 15-year tenure as head of the Royal National Theatre. As Rich notes,

> Mr. Hall's *Orpheus* [*Descending*], which opened Tuesday night [13 December 1988] at the Haymarket Theatre, may well prove a landmark. The director has not only given his fledgling company a hit and reclaimed a little-seen work that expired in two months on Broadway in 1957; he has also rethought the whole style of Williams staging. (Rich, Section C, p. 15)

Part I: Racialized Tennessee

Rethinking "the whole style," as Rich's praise of Hall suggests, has at times raised as many questions as it has answered with Williams, however, particularly in the United States. *Cat on a Hot Tin Roof* would be rethought along racial lines in America in 2008 with what *Playbill* called a "Marquee Value" African American cast featuring Anika Noni Rose as Maggie and *Hustle & Flow* film star, Terrence Howard, as Brick, beside James Earl Jones as Big Daddy and Phylicia Rachad, director Debbie Allen's sister, as Big Mama. As Professor Harvey Young noted at a 2011 roundtable on "African American Productions of Williams' Drama," "It is my understanding that the all-black *Cat* was [...] designed to appeal to audiences based upon the celebrity of the cast and crew" (Palmer, n.p.). The production played at the Broadhurst Theatre in New York from 28 February through 22 June 2009.[2] It was followed in 2012 by a Broadway revival of *A Streetcar Named Desire*, directed by Emily Mann and starring Blair Underwood, Nicole Ari Parker and Daphne Rubin-Vega in what *Playbill* called "a multi-ethnic staging," by the same producers as those for *Cat on a Hot Tin Roof*, Stephen C. Byrd and Alia M. Jones, the play opening also at the Broadhurst Theatre.

The all African American casting of *A Streetcar Named Desire* required some overt rewriting of Williams's text, however, including the producers eliminating the family name of Kowalski and much of the dialogue associated with Stanley's Polish heritage, even as that heritage would have been implicated in patterns of ethnic or racial discriminations of the time. Danusha V. Goska, for instance, maintains that "the image of the uncultured Bohunk had been depicted in popular literature before [*Streetcar*], but it entered the canon" with Williams's play, which echoed contemporary post–World War II immigration fears as it "dramatizes the racists' fear of miscegenation, and its twin conviction that America was overwhelmed by an influx of inferior others and thereby was committing 'race suicide'" (Goska 414). Rachel Van Duyvenbode, picks up the thread in "Darkness Made Visible: Miscegenation, Masquerade and the Signified Racial Other," that Blanche herself is suggesting real if coded issues of miscegenation in the relationship between Stella and Stanley. The ethnic/racial issue is further complicated as Blanche, too, is tied to the theme of Polish identity. In a note on Polish history in *Streetcar*, Philip C. Kolin reminds us that, "Blanche is also subtly linked to Polish culture and history through the *Varsouviana*, the polka or waltz, that triggers memories of her gay husband's suicide at Moon Lake and pushes her further into madness" (Kolin 2011), and so the Polish tune itself is further implicated in Blanche's sexuality. By the strictures of whiteness that dominated much of mid-twentieth-century America, which Blanche voices, eastern and southern Europeans would be deemed at very least racially dubious. Sidestepping racially charged contemporary immigration fears in which any figure with a "swarthy" complexion would be deemed not quite white by WASP America, or as Ben Brantley says in his less than flattering *New York Times* review, "eliminate all nontracking references, like Stanley's being Polish, as this version does" (April 22, 2012), his being deemed "common as dirt," Emile Mann's production at very least diminishes the episodes of Stanley's rage over his "outsider" status in an America he fought for; gone, then, is the language lesson Stanley delivers to the superior sisters on the difference between "Polack" and "Poles." He is deemed "sub-human" and likened to an ape by Blanche, and even Stella calls her husband "a different species," a phrase with racial implication.

That "different species" is visually accented on the racialized cover of the New Directions edition of the play that features three abstracted human figures, white figures, clearly female since they have stylized breasts, on either side of a black one.[3]

Such imagery further raises questions about Stanley's racial profile, but they resonate differently applied to African Americans rather than to

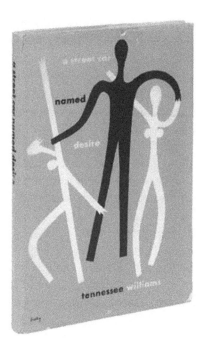

Figure 2.1 *A Streetcar Named Desire*, first edition cover design by Alvin Lustig

Polish-Americans (or Italian Americans in other Williams plays) especially in 2012. Critic George Crandell has defended such textual manipulation even before the Allen production, during the 2011 Williams symposium roundtable, what Philip C. Kolin, on the same panel, has called "enlarging the script." Crandell sees Stanley as something of an African American stand-in:

> If you look at the character of Stanley Kowalski, for example, and examine the characteristics that Williams uses to describe him, they fit some of the stereotypical views of African-Americans at the time. And so the suggestion is that Tennessee Williams may have had in mind Stanley as a black man rather than a Pole, and his efforts to assert himself or his identity are his efforts as an "other" black American; to assert himself as an American in a context that would not recognize him, that sees him [i.e., treats him] largely as invisible. (Palmer, 2011)

Invisibility seems hardly at issue with Stanley, however. Prof. Harvey Young is also comfortable with rewritings of the play, or at least defends a swerve in some productions from ethnicity to race directly:

I would like to expand on […] the role of ethnicity in Williams' work. Earlier today, there was a terrific session on the representation of Italian Americans in *The Rose Tattoo*. Similarly, I believe there's a way in which Stanley in *A Streetcar Named Desire* exists as a flattened or condensed representation of the racialized "other." He is explicitly marked as Polish but could easily be—based on his occupation and the manner with which he is regarded by Blanche—African American or Italian American within the temporal setting of the play. (Palmer, 2011)

At the same roundtable, Philip Kolin offers a strong counter to the general critical perception that Williams was inattentive to African Americans and contemporary civil-rights issues, and he cites Harry Rasky's documentary, *Tennessee Williams: A Portrait in Laughter and Lamentations*,[4] where Williams acknowledges, "I always thought I was black."

Gloria McMillan continues the race-ethnicity debate in terms of culturally permissible villainy:

Since even in Williams's time it would not have been acceptable to most audiences in larger cities to just make the villain [of *A Streetcar Named Desire*] an African American, though Stanley appears to be standing in for the hulking dark rapist threat, we need somebody who isn't one of us. Enter "the greasy Polack." The letter to Marlon Brando from Williams used the term and went on to say that Brando might ride the comet of the character all the way to "the melancholy Dane." (McMillan, 2020)

When Williams does address issues of race directly, albeit not through a major African American character, he evokes the tradition of Jim Crow segregation laws and its accompanying violence as he does in *Sweet Bird of Youth*, when Scotty paraphrases the political position of Boss Finley, whose daughter Chance Wayne has seduced and impregnated before he fled. Of Finley Scotty says, "He's going to state his position on that emasculation business that's stirred up such a mess in the state. […] Well, they picked out a nigger at random and castrated the bastard to show they mean business about white women's protection in this state." When Chance doubts the event, the bartender, Stuff, is incredulous, "You doubt they cut that Nigger?" (90). In the stage version of the play at least, Scotty describes what may become the fate of Chance as well. For Chance such brutality is driven by "sex-envy" toward African Americans. But Williams has also personally engaged with racial issues and civil rights, particularly in the 1960s. When the American Place Theatre was created in 1963 in New York's St. Clements Church as an off-Broadway theater (but in Hell's Kitchen), it was receptive to and encouraged the African American theater movement. Tennessee Williams was among its original Board of Directors.

John Lahr, on the other hand, would resist such rethinking and even rewriting of Williams along racial lines when he called for something like racial reciprocity: "no more infernal all-black productions of Tennessee Williams plays unless we can have their equal in folly: all-white productions of August Wilson," from whose objections to racial or ethnic interchangeability on stage, along with cross-cultural productions in general, which may be his or their underlying thread, Lahr takes his cue.[5] As unsettling as Lahr's phrasing of "infernal all-black productions of Tennessee Williams" is the broader reestablishment of something like an "us versus them" theatrical chasm, which "racially neutral" or "color-blind" productions struggle to bridge. Critics of Lahr have further characterized his position as a reassertion not only of otherness, a theme Williams frequently takes on, although not always through race directly, but also of white exceptionalism, and, further, objections such as Lahr's may have echoed through Broadway's theater machinery, as this high-profile, "race neutral" *Streetcar* revival was ignored at the 2012 Tony Awards, despite the extension of its Broadway run. Ben Brantley, however, may have had as much impact on that decision as Lahr as he has deemed this production a "torpid revival of the play," noting further that "this 'Streetcar' is mostly an exquisite snooze" (April 22, 2012). On the other hand, Lahr's position, knowingly or not, is compatible with what currently, in the "Black Lives Matter" moment, is called "Critical Race Theory" (CRT), which sees racism as endemic in contemporary cultures, deeply engrained in legal systems and economies. For such thinkers neutrality, objectivity, color blindness and meritocracy are camouflage; these critics challenge the ahistoricism that color blindness entails.[6] Lahr may not associate himself directly with such positions, which are often anti-universalist and finally anti-humanist and focus on the uniqueness of Blackness, but there remains a certain concord in these views.

Director Debbie Allen's updating of *Cat on a Hot Tin Roof* to the 1980s sought to diffuse at least one racial and historical issue that might further have skewed this revival had she retained Williams's setting in the heavily segregated American South under its Jim Crow laws. Nonetheless, Allen both foregrounds and potentially muddles one of the great themes of the American South that Williams himself tended to treat less directly than he might have, race relations.[7] That is, Allen stretches credibility by rendering a "redneck" Big Daddy, a former overseer, the reputations of which were generally that of ruthless and violent plantation managers, as now a Black plantation owner with his own Black servants and plantation help, $10 million to distribute, and "28,000 acres of the richest land this side of the valley Nile" up for grabs. Such amassed wealth and its social standing stretch credulity even in the play's updated 1980s setting, as they do in its 2009 performance time frame. After a limited New York run, deemed an economic success by Paul Taylor writing in London's the *Independent*, the production transferred to the Novello Theatre in London in November of 2009, with replacements Sanaa Lathan and Adrian Lester as the dysfunctional couple, where it ran until April 10, 2010.

Michael Billington's review in the *Guardian* was generous but not without its blind spots as he deflects issues with the ploy of rhetorical questions. That said, he doubtless helped increase the house even as he avoids the central issue of race in America: "What difference does it make that Tennessee Williams' play is performed by a Black cast in Debbie Allen's Broadway production? It undoubtedly gives the work a new dynamic. But ethnicity [i.e., race] matters less than emotional firepower and an awareness of the essential Williams conflict between lies and truth; and both are abundantly present in this exhilarating evening" (Billington, 2009, n.p.). Billington also avoids the "essential Williams conflict" of uncertain sexuality, which is the generating issue for much of the mendacity. That West End production, however, went on to win the 2010 Laurence Olivier Award for "Best Revival" of a play.

The Allen and Mann productions relied on the late twentieth-century theatrical convention of "color-blind," "race neutral" or, more broadly, "nontraditional casting," in which audience members were thought, taught or otherwise encouraged not to see race (subsequently gender or ability) on stage. But the lessons of "color-blind casting" (sometimes "reverse casting," as in some productions with a white Othello as part of an otherwise Black cast) have tended to work better with mixed-race productions, that is, with integration, as in the confusions over two sets of identical but racially mixed twins in Shakespeare's *A Comedy of Errors*, or, in fact, in the less-than-high-profile Nashville Repertory Theatre's 2020 revival of *A Streetcar Named Desire* (just before the world theater pandemic lock down), directed by Ned McIntyre with an African American Stella in an otherwise white cast.[8] In the roundtable symposium cited above, Kolin noted that, "in 1983, a Creole production was done by Charles Gordone, the first African American to win the Pulitzer in drama, featuring a black Stanley with a white Blanche, raising again all kinds of sociopolitical issues in the script." That is, this Stanley, too, would have "issues" with a Polish surname and heritage. Such expanding of the Williams script, Kolin adds in its defense, is how "we get away from the idea of cultural encoding: that there are certain actors that can play certain parts. Blanche is always the southern belle, Stanley always the Pole, but in many African American productions of these plays these cultural encodings have been disrupted."

The convention of racial "blindness" is often more difficult to credit with a mono-racial cast in which one is asked to be blind to race in the Pollitt family itself, the patriarch of which Billington accurately describes as a "domestic tyrant," on the one hand, but to treat it as conspicuous among the underclass of that social structure, the Pollitt servants and farm workers over whom this "domestic tyrant" also rules, on the other. The assertion, at least theatrically, of a "post-racial" world, may also entail or necessitate a "post historical" perspective or to require at least a certain cultural amnesia. Paul Taylor (2009) lays out his version of the convention: "What is remarkable, though, about Allen's compelling, sensitive and acerbically comic production is how swiftly you become so absorbed by the universal elements in the story that you almost completely forget about the counter-intuitive colour of the actors' skins." Taylor, thus, lays out the goal of "color-blind casting," but his "almost completely forget" may need some unpacking for the level of cultural amnesia or suspended history necessary among his projected "you" as his comment sidesteps or brackets the cultural and economic divide that continues to separate the races in the United States, which the integration movements of the 1950s and 1960s have, finally, failed to bridge or otherwise overcome.

Theater professionals have continued to work toward those goals that Taylor outlines, in particular during the 2020 pandemic that closed theaters. Audra McDonald, of whom Michael Schulman of the *New Yorker* has said that her, "Carrie Pipperidge in a Lincoln Center revival of 'Carousel,' […] was hailed as a breakthrough in 'color-blind casting,' and [for which she] won her first Tony Award for the role." She was scheduled to play Blanche DuBois at the famed Williamstown, Massachusetts, Theater Festival in the summer of 2020 as part of an integrated, "color-blind" production. As McDonald noted, "I chose to do this specific production of 'Streetcar' […] because Robert O'Hara is directing it. So this is a Black man directing this iconic piece of theatre and doing something quite revolutionary with it."[9] On the issue of "color-blind casting" McDonald notes directly that the issue is not just color, but interpretation, a rethinking of "the whole style," an expansion of the script:

> Yeah, and instead of just saying, "We've slipped them in, and, look at that, they're doing just as well as a white person in that role," it's, like, "No, they're in this role for a very specific reason," to either blow the interpretation out in a completely different way or shine a light on who these characters are. The whole context of the play has to be in some ways reimagined, because you're not saying, "Be blind to their color." You're saying, "Let their color now enhance how you see this entire story." (Schulman, 2020)

Free People of Color

Admittedly, "free people of color" did exist for a time in North America, and some of those owned plantations, particularly in territories that would finally become the United States in 1803, and American playwright John Guare has explored and detailed some of those issues in his 2010 play, *Free Man of Color*, set in a New Orleans of 1801, which, at that time was an integrated international city where free humans of every race and creed enjoyed almost unrestricted freedoms. Its main character, Jacques Cornet, is "a new world Don Juan" who is the wealthiest man of color in New Orleans; technically a mulatto,[10] his wealth was acquired through his father who is a major plantation owner. That theatrical moment might be seen as something of a validation for the racial transformation of *Cat on a Hot Tin Roof*, but wealth in *Free Man of Color* is a corrupting influence associated with and, indeed, enabling political corruption, immorality and debauchery, and the city's international status with its social freedoms essentially vanished with the Louisiana Purchase with the reintroduction of color lines and the system of enslavement two years later. "Free men of color" remains a phrase deeply submerged, historically and culturally, in the American psyche, and the almost concurrent production of an all-Black *Cat on a Hot Tin Roof* is set as a contemporary reality rather than an historical depiction.

On the other hand, what needed little rethinking, rewriting, expansion or updating, on either side of the Atlantic, are classic Williams themes. Billington cites one as "the essential Williams conflict between lies and truth," to which Brick offers the counter, self-reflexive riposte, "mendacity is the system that we live in," punctuating his comment with, "Liquor is one way out and death's the other." What plays less well in such rethinking, however, is Williams's more frequent issue, something of the passing of the old and segregated order, what might generally be called the residue of a plantation social structure that depended for its social hierarchies on slaves, and later on hordes of sharecroppers, plantation help and underpaid household servants that still haunts the Southern American legacy. Servants—owned, indentured or salaried—formed the bulwark not only of the so-called and vanishing aristocratic South (see William Faulkner and Eudora Welty, for instance) but of middle-class life through and beyond the Civil Rights Movement and the overt demise of Jim Crow, and those servants and household help were dominantly African Americans (with on occasion immigrant labor). That post-Louisiana Purchase, slavery-supported plantation system and its persistent residue through twentieth- and twenty-first-century middle-class Southern life are difficult to erase from history. It is one thing to put the sex back into Williams in the UK, as Davies apparently did with his *Cat on a Hot Tin Roof* revival, quite another to be as blind to the dominant strain of the American ethos as Mann was.

Admittedly, by 2008, another kind of history seems to have caught up with Williams, as even a rethought play becomes something of a paradox, a period piece in a new, uncertain century, a quaint anachronism that Mann's partial updating is at a loss to address. Caroline Kellet Fraysse summarizes such cultural change:

> This *Cat on a Hot Tin Roof* is dissipated by history's diminution of its central controversies. In the homosexual playwright's day, the proclivities he infers [i.e., implies] in the text were illegal, and our own Lord Chamberlain banned the production [see below]. Furthermore, the delicate topic of cancer remained secretive, and alcoholism was still a misunderstood taboo.

What were restricted topics and shocking medical avoidance and ignorance of the 1950s, both part of the world in which Williams came of age and themes that his contemporary censors were eager to delete, are neither provocative nor shocking in the twenty-first century. To continue to make Williams's work contemporary, producers, directors and actors need to plumb those depths in Williams that still resonate, and many have, as Rich suggests.

Part II: Anglicizing Williams, London's Post–World War II Theater Climate

London's post–World War II era was another matter. In his 1997 reminiscence, director Peter Hall writes of another opportunity that arose from his early struggles with the Lord Chamberlain over his staging the English-language premiere of Samuel Beckett's *Waiting for Godot*:

> One morning the phone rang and a gentle voice from the South announced improbably that it belonged to Tennessee Williams. He had seen *Godot* and wished to meet me. He gave me the rights to direct his plays in London. (Hall)

The phone call would launch another series of battles between the Lord Chamberlain and Hall as the director went on to stage Williams's less culturally controversial but phantasmagoric play, *Camino Real*, at the Phoenix Theatre in 1957 without incident, but the more controversial, since unexpurgated, production of *Cat on a Hot Tin Roof* needed to be staged at the Comedy Theatre

Figure 2.2 The New Watergate Theatre Club, *Cat on a Hot Tin Roof* cast list

functioning as a private club theater and so was presented "by subterfuge" in 1958 (Kolin, 1998, 104).[11] Such restrictions on public performance created something of a paradox according to the *Guardian* critic Philip Hope-Wallace, writing on January 31, 1958, since *Cat on a Hot Tin Roof*

> can be bought on any bookstall in the Penguin edition, [but] is nevertheless a banned play and was last night put on by subterfuge as a club theatre production at the Watergate Theatre Club.[12]

> Such censorship may look fatuous and hypocritical but, if the facade serves as a filter to keep out the shockable, it is not so foolish a device. For this play is in a true sense shocking. It has a violence of utterance beyond anything else Mr Williams has written, and it is about sawn-off, coarse, violent people, often seen with a savage veracity but not, as in some of Williams' other plays, winning much sympathy. (Hope-Wallace, 1958)

As the British Library's censorship blog notes,

whilst the Lord Chamberlain's Office could ban a play from public performance, it had no jurisdiction over private performances which could take place in "private" theatres often established as club theatres where access was granted to audiences who paid a nominal subscription to the club. *Cat on a Hot Tin Roof* was first performed "privately" in Britain for The New Watergate Club at The Comedy Theatre in January 1958. Founded with the intention of staging plays without censorship, the club boasted 64,000 members at the time of the play's premiere and helped undermine the authority of the Lord Chamberlain's Office enabling plays with LGBTQ content to be performed uncensored. (British Library, 2019)

At the Lord Chamberlain's Office

The first query for Hall's production of *Cat on a Hot Tin Roof* came from London's Arts Theatre on October 29, 1955, sent by Anne Jenkins, the theater's manager. The Lord Chamberlain's report was quickly issued by Examiner of Plays, C. D. Heriot, on November 2, 1955. Williams's reputation preceding him, however, and Heriot's assessment contained the following damning appraisal:

> Once again Mr. Williams vomits up the recurring theme of his not-too-subconscious. This is the fourth play (and there are sure to be others) where we are confronted by the gentlewoman debased, sunk in her private dreams as a remedy for her sexual frustration, and over all [is] the author's horror, disgust and rage against the sexual act. [...]

> Two versions of the last act are submitted. In the first, and original version, the family bicker and quarrel in the absence of the father, until Margaret suddenly announces the fact that she is pregnant—this insuring that she and Brick will inherit the larger part (if not the whole) of the estate—and at the very end of the play, hiding all the bottles of drink from Brick and telling him that if he wants one, he must impregnate her first.

> The second version of the last act is the one in which the producer, Elia Kazan, collaborated with the author for the New York production. It is sentimental and false. Margaret's announcement is made in the presence of the father amid a symbolic thunderstorm, the brother and sister in law are foiled of their share of the estate and Margaret dramatically splinters all the drink bottles on the concrete below the veranda, while Brick sheepishly remembers his manhood. There is an

added and unnecessary incident story about elephants. (See Parker on these issues)

The whole thing is pretentious, over-strained, and hysterical. The author obviously believes he is writing Literature with a big L. (An example of his pretentiousness can be seen on page 46 of Act II). The language is repetitively coarse—and loses its effect in consequence.

As far as I can judge, the homosexual element is false—that is to say, we are to believe Brick when he says that his wife and relations "dreamed it up." I think, therefore, that with a lot of cuts, listed below, the Lord Chamberlain might consider granting a license for this bogus play. ("Homosexuality, Censorship and the British Stage," 2019)

Cat on a Hot Tin Roof was resubmitted to the Lord Chamberlain on December 1, 1958, and submitted yet again, now by the Connaught Theatre of Worthing, on July 8, 1959; re-reviewing the play on July 12, 1963, Heriot cites the submissions "in 1955 and 1958" (see above) licenses for which could not finally be issued "because there was no time or place of production" and so "no license was issued." Such persistent and adamant licensing denials were made in the face of "this bogus play," this "pretentious, over-strained, and hysterical" work's having won not only the Pulitzer Prize for Drama in the United States in 1955 (Williams's second, after *A Streetcar Named Desire* received the award in 1948), but in the UK, Hall's club production won the *London Evening Standard* Theatre Award for 1958.

Other European countries found Williams less toxic:

Gothenburg City Theatre [Stockholm …] hosted the lucrative European premiere of *Cat on a Hot Tin Roof* in September 1955.

Apart from the numerous regional theatres where Williams' plays were frequently performed, his works found a welcoming home at the private Vasa Theatre in Stockholm (which enjoyed record box-office success with a production of *Cat* in 1956, and hosted the European premiere of *Sweet Bird of Youth* in 1959). […]

On two separate occasions, Williams paid a visit to Sweden in order to attend the European premieres of *The Rose Tattoo* in 1951 and *Cat on a Hot Tin Roof* in 1955, both at Gothenburg City Theatre. The latter production was significantly more sexually daring than Elia Kazan's Broadway version and notable for its lead actress Gunnel Broström as Maggie Pollitt, who played the major part of the first act in nothing but a bra and panties (unlike Barbara Bel Geddes on Broadway, who wore a less-revealing slip during these scenes). The production, which also offered a rather exoticized view of the Deep South, mesmerized Swedish audiences and critics and precipitated a media debate over the representation of female sexuality, which continued for several months following opening night.

Despite Williams' own doubts about the merits of the Gothenburg production, "done so badly that I could hardly sit through it" [St. Juste, 127] as he (arguably unfairly) dismissed it, he approached Schmidt the following year with a request to produce *Cat on a Hot Tin Roof* in Paris, a market that up until then had been less than embracing of both his own plays and American drama in general. In December 1956, for instance, the same month that *Cat* opened in the French capital, the influential magazine *Arts* published a long condemnation of American theatre, which it deemed to be melodramatic, predictable, and spiced up with "eroticism or perversity, sadism or drugs." (Gindt 2013, 26)[13]

"The Start of Modern Drama"

In his historical retrospect, Hall has dated "the start of modern drama" from this 1950s period, that is, not just "modern [British] drama" but "modern drama." He does so not with the landmark staging of John Osborne's *Look Back in Anger* by the English Stage Company in 1956.[14] Instead, he begins a year earlier with *his* staging of *Waiting for Godot*, in August of 1955, to which we might further add his daring *Cat on a Hot Tin Roof* in 1958 to create something like an internationalist trilogy of modern twentieth-century drama, tetralogy if we add the English Stage Company's production of *Orpheus Descending*, directed by Tony Richardson in May 1959. What Hall avoids or ignores, however, are two seminal Williams productions that paved the way for much theatrical change in the UK. The first was the West End production of Tennessee Williams's *The Glass Menagerie* at the Theatre Royal Haymarket, directed by John Gielgud. The Original Broadway production opened on March 31, 1945, at the Playhouse Theatre in New York City and ran for 563 performances. The London production opened July 28th, 1948 and ran for 109 performances with Helen Hayes, making her London debut, Frances Heflin, Phil Brown and Hugh Mc Dermott. Original music was composed by Paul Bowles with sets by Jo Mielziner. It was produced by Tennent Productions, Ltd. in association with the Arts Council of Great Britain and by arrangement with the Theater Guild of New York, which suggests that it followed closely the New York production.

The second was Laurence Olivier's staging of *A Streetcar Named Desire*, with his wife, at the time, Vivien Leigh, as Blanche, which opened in London's West End on October 11, 1949, and ran at the Aldwych Theatre for 326 performances.

The productions of the two plays above suggest that Hall's dating of modernity and the drama, particularly in the UK, may be off by at least a full decade, his timeline thus a bit self-serving. While *The Glass Menagerie* was staged in London without much resistance, *Streetcar*'s route to the West End was contentious and fraught with obstacles as the British premiere ran up against the remnants of Victorianism amid the austerities of a post–World War II Britain's reestablishing its identity, which censorship Philip Hope-Wallace (above) continued to justify. *A Streetcar Named Desire* was met with primarily moral resistance if not hostility from newspapers like the *Sunday Pictorial* (5 million in circulation) as well, which, on October 2, 1949, called the play "salacious and degrading" (Kolin, 2000, 62). When Leigh was chosen to play Blanche for the British premiere, she agreed on condition that her husband, Lawrence Olivier, direct, a condition quickly agreed, after which Olivier became co-producer as well.[15] And although the English production was not an exact copy of the New York staging, a substantial level of

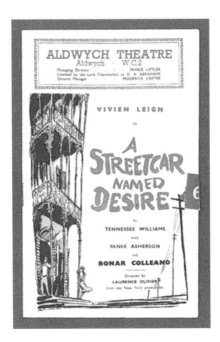

Figure 2.3 Program for *A Streetcar Named Desire*, "Directed by Laurence Olivier from the New York Production"

reproduction was inevitable since the New York production made so strong an international impact, what Gore Vidal famously called "an earthquake" (Vidal cited in Lahr, 2014, 146). Needless to say, the diluted UK production produced no such temblors even as Olivier received and used Elia Kazan's prompt books so that the production finally looked and sounded much like that in New York. Moreover, Olivier also used Joseph 'Jo' Mielziner's sets, Alex North's music, the advertising imagery mimicked almost exactly that of the New York production (as above),[16] the playbill finally acknowledging, "Directed by Lawrence Olivier from the New York production." The British staging was, however, considerably shortened and substantially censored.

The license to perform was applied for in 1948, granted only, after protracted negotiation, in October 1949 with extensive cuts, including Stanley's reference to his "kidneys" (102) suffering from Blanche's extended use of the apartment's only toilet. Further, Olivier was warned by the Lord Chamberlain's office, "no suggestive business accompanying any undressing." Olivier accepted such sanitizing, but he also sent Williams his own redrafting of the play, a 16-page, handwritten letter[17] with suggested cuts and changes for the London opening, many designed to deal with what some critics attending the Manchester Opera House try-outs, from September 27 to October 7, 1949, considered the play's excessive length, what Olivier would call scenes, "dangerously loaded with length," offering in the process a writing tutorial to the playwright: "It is highly dangerous to have an early scene between two people like Stella and Blanche seem long" (Kolin, 2000, 151). He also offered a "new reading" of Stanley as "not the bruiser type," Olivier generally defending this new reading to the playwright as "a slightly subtler approach" that added a claimed vitality to the play, but finally modulated it. Essentially, Olivier was rewriting the play and Williams's Stanley in particular for his male lead and his British audience unaccustomed to such tectonic slippages as Williams had on offer. Looking back on the issues in 1974, Williams famously quipped that anyone who writes so detailed a letter deserves respect, so he acceded to Olivier's cuts and revisions, many of which copied and justified those mandated by the Lord Chamberlain. Other suggestions were based on Olivier's work with the play in its Manchester try-out and the nature of his leading actors. The result was an overall reduction of the play's running time by nearly an hour, from three hours (with two intervals)[18] in Manchester to just over two hours in London, and so it was not until the renewed interest in Williams in the 1980s (cited by Rich, 1988) that Britain's theater audiences finally saw the complete play, since the American film, available in the UK in 1952, was itself heavily censored.

Olivier seems to have got Williams wrong again, this time as an actor when he played Big Daddy in a 90-minute, truncated version of *Cat on a Hot Tin Roof* for British television in 1976.[19] According to Billington, writing in 2012,

The author wasn't much more thrilled with a 1976 Granada TV production, starring Natalie Wood and Robert Wagner. Here, according to Williams, Laurence Olivier mistakenly conceived Big Daddy as "a southern planter gentleman instead of a former overseer who struck it rich through hard work." In fact, you have to leap forward to 1988 to find a British production that finally did full justice to Williams' symphonic play. This was Howard Davies's superlative revival at the National Theatre [cited by Rich, 1988 above], starring Lindsay Duncan as Maggie, Ian Charlson as Brick and Eric Porter as Big Daddy. (Williams cited in Billington, 2012)

Billington here seems to be echoing Kolin as well, who, two years earlier, writing in the 2010 Methuen Drama edition of the play, noted more pointedly that "Olivier looked more like a stately elder Mark Twain or slimmer Colonel Sanders projecting an aristocratic Big Daddy, not the self-made, coarse man Williams imagined" (Williams, 2010, lxii–lxiii).

Olivier's "new reading" of Stanley Kowalski's character in 1949 did not, mercifully, establish a standard for staging in the UK, despite Olivier's claim that his re-rendering added vitality to the play. As Michael Billington wrote in reference to Benedict Andrews's updated, heavily sexualized, if at times also anachronistic, revival of the play at the Young Vic in March of 2014,

> Ben Foster […] plays Stanley as a deeply physical man whose natural instinct when crossed is to lash out. There is something dangerous about this sweaty, tattooed, close-cropped Stanley who has recently been discharged from the military and who has not lost his combative instinct. At the same time, you understand his refusal to be patronised and insulted by his affected sister-in-law. (Billington, 2014)

The *Daily Mail* called Foster's Stanley, "chillingly thuggish" (cited in advertising). Billington's appraisal returns to Kenneth Tynan's observation of Olivier's (censored) production and the theatrical change generated in post–World War II Britain, "For the first time in its history, English theatre has been swayed and shaped by America, by which I mean Hollywood as well as Broadway. The young people […] cut their teeth on the films of Welles, Wyler, Wilder and Kazan and on the plays (later adapted for the screen) of Arthur Miller and Tennessee Williams" (Tynan cited in Shellard, 2003, 245). Billington's assessment punctuates such cross-fertilization, the two-way transatlantic traffic by 2014 detailed by Frank Rich.

Hall was less tolerant of British theatrical repression and the Lord Chamberlain's demanding cuts with his 1958 production of *Cat on a Hot*

Tin Roof. His "subversive" solution was to repeat his initial 1955 strategy for Samuel Beckett's *Waiting for Godot*, also a victim of the Lord Chamberlain's blue pencil: circumvention, the play performed at a private club, which put the performance beyond the reach of the Lord Chamberlain, although Hall, too, would accede to the Lord Chamberlain's demands for the Beckett premiere once the show was moved to the West End.

The Lord Chamberlain's Blue Pencil

An exhibit at the Harry Ransom Humanities Research Center at the University of Texas in Austin celebrating the Williams centenary in 2011 and called "Becoming Tennessee Williams,"[20] offered an overview of not only Williams's difficulties with the censors, American and European, but Hall's as well. Guy Adams, writing for London's *Independent* also in 2011, summarizes the long list of cuts and request for alterations that Olivier and Hall received:

> *Streetcar* was eventually staged, with Laurence Olivier as a director, in 1949, two years after it had opened on Broadway. But an effort to bring *Cat on a Hot Tin Roof* to the UK almost a decade later met even more severe difficulties. A 1955 letter from the Lord Chamberlain—part of a collection at the Harry Ransom Center at the University of Texas— reveals that the producers were told to make 34 changes to the script before it was deemed acceptable for London.
>
> Williams was told to delete allegedly offensive words, including "crap," "Christ," "Jesus," "bull crap," "frig," "half ass," "boobs," "humping" and "ass-aching." He was also told to cut a paragraph in which a character discusses a sexual liaison by saying: "I laid her, regular as a piston."
>
> [...] instructions to remove entire pages that referred to the homosexuality of Brick. [...] Phrases such as "ducking sissies" and "queers" had to be cut. A typical paragraph [of the report] reads: "The discussion on page 45[21] [must] be altered, so as to eliminate the suggestion that there may have been a homosexual relationship." (Adams, 2011, n.p.)

The response to *Cat on a Hot Tin Roof* thus almost duplicated the Lord Chamberlain's required alterations to *A Streetcar Named Desire* a decade earlier. *A Streetcar Named Desire* was submitted for license by H. M. Tennent for the Globe Theatre on Shaftsbury Avenue on June 23, 1948, with the requisite reading fee of 2 pounds 2 shillings. The results were sent by N. W. Gwatkin to William Conway on July 12, 1948. What was read was a mimeographed copy, stamped June 24, 1948, the multiple copies made by the well-regarded "Mrs. Marshall's Typewriting Service" in The Strand, a member of "The Society of Typists," that is, a "Play Typists" service that Oscar Wilde used as well. In June of 1949 the following comments were made on the Lord Chamberlain's copy:

I-2-13 marked for cut: "The four-letter word deprived us of our plantation."

I-3-2 "for the sake of Jesus" altered to "for god's sake"

I-3-6 "Well, one night—the plaster cracked!" marked as questionable. [Retained]

I-4-9 "But there are things that happen between a man and a woman in the dark"; "in the dark" marked as questionable with the question "leave?"

II-1-3 "That ruttin' hunk" marked "alter everywhere" and a request for "euphemism"

II-1-5 "I only do that with other girls because I love you"; "do that" marked for cutting; "fool with" offered as an alternative.

II-2-3 "In fact I was somewhat flattered that—desired me!"; "desired me" questioned with the note "seems unnecessary." Another comment "I should leave [it]."

II-2-4 Marked for cut all of Blanche's French with Mitch.

II-2-10 "Then I found out. In the worst of all possible ways." Good deal of marginalia erased, but "for his negress" offered as a possibility; "and another" offered as well. To "Afterwards we pretended that nothing had been discovered. Yes, the three of us drove out to Moon Lake Casino"; "the three of us" cut and a "we" substituted.

III-1-6 "It's not my soul, it's my kidneys I'm worried about"; one comment "Pity to cut this but I suppose we should"

III-1-7 "This beautiful and talented young man was a degenerate" marked for cutting.

III-2-2 "God damns" left here unaltered.

III-2-4 "God, honey, it's gonna be sweet when we can make noise in the night the way we used to and get the colored lights going with nobody's sister behind the curtains to hear us." Note: "This I gather is an elaborate euphemism, which I should leave" is the comment.

III-3-5 "Christ" changed to "God"

III-5-1 and III-5-11"ruttin'" cut. (Olivier Archive)[22]

The Lord Chamberlain's Reader's Report of June 25, 1948, was followed by the Lord Chamberlain's stamp dated April 13, 1949, apparently the date of approval. *Streetcar* was described in the reports as "a mixture of the lurid and the high-brow," a play about "a tragic nymphomaniac." The approval came with a general "warning about undressing." While "there is nothing in the story that would justify a ban" and "nothing insuperable over production of the play, there are also a number of god-damns, but they have already typed some of them with the 'god' [set off] in brackets [as an alternative], and so [the producers] are no doubt ready to modify them accordingly," the comments including the note, read by H. C. Game referencing Allardyce Nicoll. Another handwritten note on the script emphasized, "cut ruttin' everywhere" and was part of the call to issue "a general warning to Tennent that they must see that reasonable restraint is exercised in production to suit the (still) milder tastes of an English audience compared to the American." The Assistant Comptroller for the Lord Chamberlain writes (to Tennent presumably) agreeing with Game's recommendations, adding further specificity:

> Act 2, scene 2, p. 10, the passage from "Then I found out. In the worst of all possible ways" down to "the three of us drove out to Moon Lake Casion [*sic*]," on p. 11. The Lord Chamberlain is of the opinion that this passage should be altered, making the young man found with a negress, instead of another man. This would entail altering or omitting, the lines on page 7, Act III, scene 1, "This beautiful and talented young man was a degenerate." (Olivier Archive)

Olivier conceded, in a letter of October 6, 1949, on behalf of Laurence Olivier Productions, Limited, written from the Midland Hotel, Manchester, to Brigadier Norman Gwatkin, acknowledging the LC's cuts and agreeing that the Lord Chamberlain's "Endorsement" depended on the following alterations:

1. Act 1, scene 2, p. 13 "The four-letter word" is out [That is, this phrase, not any particular "four-letter word"],
2. Act 1, scene 2, p. 13 "for God's sake" is substituted for "for the sake of Jesus,"

3. All use of the word "ruttin'" is omitted,

4. Act 2, scene 1, p. 5 "fool with" is substituted for "do that,"

5. Act 2, scene 2, p. 11 "an older man who had been his friend for years" is omitted,

6. Act 3, scene 1, p. 6 You kindly allowed me to have "It's not my soul I'm worried about" cutting the words "it's my kidneys" from the sentence,

7. Act 3, scene 3, p. 6 "God" is substituted for "Christ,"

8. All the undressing business is conducted in a perfectly wholesome domestic manner,

9. Over and above these points, you allowed me to include:

> Act 1, scene 1 The following joke told by Steve: "And the old lady is on her way to Mass and she's late and there's a cop standin' in front of th' church an' she comes runnin' up an' says 'Officer—is Mass out yet?' He looks her over and says 'No, Lady, but y'r hat is on crooked!'" There is a great deal of business accompanying this dialogue and the point of the story receives no mark of appreciation from the audience. It is, however, helpful as a piece of character and mood setting[.]

> Act 2, scene 1, p. 3. "that dribble puss hunk" as alternative to "ruttin'."

> Act 3, scene 5, p. 1. Pablo: "I'm cursing your <u>Godamn</u> luck," in place of "ruttin'."

> Signed L. Olivier.[23]

Hugh Beaumont, writing for producer H. M. Tennent on April 6, 1949, suggests further:

> I have now talked at length to Tennessee Williams and Irene Selznick[24] in New York and read them your latest suggestions. Both Mr. Williams and Mrs. Selznick are very upset in view of the fact that the play has now been running for over 18 months in New York, for nearly a year in Chicago, and has been produced in most of the European capitals with great success, and in no instance has any member of the American or European press raised any unfavourable comment upon the particular scene in question [Grey's suicide], or indeed upon the nature of the play.

> Tennessee Williams feels that the speech under discussion is the entire basis of "Blanche's character."[25]

Much of the popular British press was, however, unkind, particularly the *Sunday Pictorial* of October 2, 1949 (7), where in "*A Streetcar Named Desire,*" Ralph Champion notes:

> For three hours last week [i.e., the long version], I felt like a Peeping Tom. [...] instead of sitting in the stalls of a Manchester theatre, I seemed to be peering through the window of a bed-sitter in New Orleans watching with fascinated horror the intimacies of a bunch of sub-humans. [...]
>
> The censor made some cuts before the play received his blessing. Apart from occasional lines, there remain few verbal shocks. (Olivier Archive)

Harold Hobson, on the other hand, defended the play in the *Sunday Times*, November 13, 1949, along curiously moralistic grounds:

> It is strictly, and even puritanically, moral. [...] Mr. Tennessee Williams' play, far from being daring, is rigidly, even timidly, conventional [...] the wages of sin is death. [...] Mr. Williams looking into Blanche with inflexible judgement but also with human pity, legitimately finds in her story many moments of touching beauty. (Olivier Archive)

Creative Frisson

Such cultural friction and resistance, seemed to fuel Williams's creativity rather than dampen it, even as he often languished in self-doubt. Williams ranks among those writers whose work is difficult to separate from their personality, and his self-doubt was legendary. It comes as little surprise then that during the writing and staging of the play that treats closeted homosexuality and not so much mental illness itself as period treatment of it most directly, *Suddenly, Last Summer*, Williams himself was undergoing analysis with New York psychiatrist Dr. Lawrence Kubie, and mostly resenting the experience. As he wrote to Maria St. Just on October 30, 1957:[26]

> The analysis is still going on, and it gets a bit dreary. It can be an awful drag, concentrating so thoroughly, day after day, on all the horrid things about yourself. If only we could turn up something nice. [...] Of course he is attacking my sex life and has succeeded in destroying my interest in all except the Horse [or 'Little Horse,' Williams's nickname for his lover, Frank Merlo, named, presumably, for his teeth]. (St. Just, 1990, 150)[27]

Kubie seemed determined to cure Williams of what was perhaps the source of his creativity, as the playwright was suffering not only from his usual self-doubt but also from a number of professional setbacks during this period. The psychiatrist even suggested that Williams give up writing, which was Williams's life. *A Streetcar Named Desire*, starring Jessica Tandy in 1947, and *Cat on a Hot Tin Roof*, first staged on Broadway in 1955 with Barbara Bel Geddes in the title role, became instant classics, the latter reputedly Williams's favorite play, and both were made into highly successful films, albeit with different leading ladies and a new leading man for *Cat on A Hot Tin Roof*. *Orpheus Descending*, which British revival Rich cites above, also derives from this early period. It was a rewrite not only of the Orpheus myth but also of an earlier Williams failed play from 1940 called *Battle of Angels*, which was professionally produced but had closed on its opening night in Boston after an onstage fire emptied the theater.[28] The New York run of *Battle of Angels* was subsequently canceled, and its rewrite as *Orpheus Descending* was something of a flop on Broadway with its overload of Williams's Southern Gothic themes and imagery. Its principal actors, Maureen Stapleton, playing "the part I meant for Anna [Magnani]" (St. Just, 1990, 141), and Cliff Robertson were praised by New York critics, but the play ran for only two months, from March 21 to May 18, 1957. Of Magnani, who was scheduled to play the stage version of Lady, Williams wrote on January 3, 1957, "Deal fell through because of her unwillingness to play more than two months." The 1959 film version, directed by Sidney Lumet and now renamed *The Fugitive Kind*, fared better in part because of the casting of Marlon Brando as Val and Magnani as Lady. And the 1990 TV version of Peter Hall's 1988–89 London and New York stagings, cited by Rich above, with Venessa Redgrave and Kevin Anderson, and using the title of the stage play, was also well received. The paperback publication of the play in 1960 was not so straightforward, however. The text published is that of the Broadway play of 1957, but it was issued under the film's title and the eight pages of interior photographs and the cover art were taken from the film not from the stage performance. After the 1957 failures of *Orpheus Descending*, however, Williams turned immediately to another mythic theme and wrote *Suddenly, Last Summer* (1958), which ends with the recollected scenes of repressed homosexual rape and cannibalism reminiscent of *The Bacchae*.

Much of Williams's creative uncertainty, something of a self-analysis, is laid out in a letter to Gadge, a nickname of Elia Kazan, on April 3, 1957: "I have been living for years with an always partially and sometimes completely blocked talent, which was only quite free in *Streetcar* and for the very special reason that I thought I was dying, and that thought eclipsed the anxiety which had always blocked my talent" (Williams, 2006, 645–46). He went on to question the Broadway production of *Orpheus* directed by Harold Clurman:

> Am I wrong in thinking that if you had directed *Orpheus* it would have been one of our greatest successes? I don't think so. I think your appreciation of its basic truth would have inspired me to lift it above its theatricalism [the complaint leveled against the play by critic Walter Kerr in his review for *The New York Herald Tribune*, 22 March 1957] [...]. You could have staged the ending so it would play and score. You would have found the key in which the play is written, not just intellectually but with the artist's and poet's vision, and gotten a stunning performance from Maureen [Stapleton] all the way through. (Williams, 2006, 646)

Williams then offers himself some advice, announcing his return to New Orleans, to cut down on his drinking and to "start analysis there if I still feel I need it." The reliance of Williams on Kazan is perhaps nowhere more evident than in the staging of *Cat on a Hot Tin Roof* in March of 1955. The 1958 paperback publication includes two-third acts, the one Williams originally wrote and the one "As Played in New York Production" (Williams, 1958, 124). In a "Note of Explanation" to this second of the two third acts, Williams acknowledges the influence of a powerful director like Kazan: "I wanted Kazan to direct the play, and though these suggestions were not made in the form of an ultimatum, I was fearful that I would lose his interest if I didn't re-examine the script from his point of view. I did" (Williams, 1958, 125).

Writing in the *New York Times* on November 2, 2003, Jason Zinoman cites Kenneth Tynan's comments on the original New York production:

> When the legendary theater critic Kenneth Tynan saw the 1955 Broadway premiere of "Cat on a Hot Tin Roof," directed by Elia Kazan, he thought something was amiss. "It was August, all right, and turbulent, but there were moments of unaccountable wrongness, as if a kazoo had intruded into a string quartet," he wrote in an essay for *Mademoiselle* magazine.
>
> Tynan discovered the source of his discontent when he compared Tennessee Williams' original 1954 script with the Broadway version, which included a revamped third act, with changes recommended by Kazan. "The kazoo," Tynan wrote, "was Kazan."
>
> Kazan had encouraged Williams to soften the play's bleak conclusion for a Broadway audience. (Zinoman, 2003)

The published record of this collaboration suggests almost two different plays, a situation that rankled Williams. In an exchange of letters with Peter Brook in 1956 Williams addressed the issue forthrightly. Brook wrote:

Of course I am thrilled and delighted as I have always longed to do one of your plays. I will endeavour to do it as best as I can—will you in exchange please do something for me? Just write down at random any thoughts, comments, ideas, reactions, criticisms, etc. that have crossed your mind in connection with the New York production, the performance of the play in general, the characters, the background and so on. [29]

Williams, excited by the prospect, replied:

I have always wanted to see a play of mine produced by you, and I will put everything else aside and fly over to see this one if you will open with my own third act, I mean as I originally conceived and wrote it, but there is no point in my seeing it again in the form that doesn't have the intense honesty that I think is the play's chief virtue. (Brown, 2014)

The play he would take up after the eventual failure of *Orpheus Descending* would feature a return to New Orleans, to the city's Garden District, the title he gave his diptych that included *Suddenly, Last Summer* as one of its panels. Here Williams returned to his core themes, the repressed homosexuality that triggered cuts to early British productions of his work, particularly to *A Streetcar Named Desire* and *Cat on a Hot Tin Roof,* until the abolition of the censoring function of the Lord Chamberlain in 1968, and so he regenerated the frisson of what then might have been termed forbidden love or desire. The first reading of *Suddenly, Last Summer* by the Lord Chamberlain's office in 1958 denied production rights, the initial reviewer noting that "T. Williams has a mind like a sewer" and so "[I] shall not recommend the play for license." Cutting was not an option since eliminating references to homosexuality in the play would be like "cutting the story of Sodom and Gomorrah out of the Bible." That initial negative ruling was overturned internally, however:

I do not think it calls for banning. The only question is whether the two references to homosexuality should be deleted. They are very indirect— in fact barely recognizable as homosexual references. They are part of the tale not action. This part of the tale is an essential part of the play and I think it is a question of banning the whole play or allowing it all.

I will allow it all and a license can be issued. (The Lord Chamberlain Archive)

Part III: Summary

The world around Williams in the 1960s and 1970s was changing at an astonishing pace, the cultural revolution of the period rendering most of his themes of sexual closeting and repression almost inconsequential. At least the entrenched cultural taboos against which he wrote seem to have disappeared by the mid-1960s and 1970s. Broadway productions of his work grew infrequent, while those mounted tended to have short runs. The exceptions relied on star power for their draw, like the 1990 revival of *Cat on a Hot Tin Roof* with Kathleen Turner as Maggie the Cat, Daniel Hugh Kelly as Brick and Charles Durning as Big Daddy in Howard Davies's Broadway restaging of his 1988 London success. Somehow, by the 1980s, Williams's plays seem to resonate more fully, even in America, with European directors willing to probe the subtleties of their psychological depths, even as Williams himself seems to have acknowledged not only that attitudes toward sexuality, particularly homosexuality, his principal taboo, had changed drastically over his creative lifetime but also that theater itself was moving in new directions. After the very limited success of *The Night of the Iguana* in 1962, he mused to an interviewer from *Theatre Arts*, "I think my kind of literary or pseudo-literary style of writing for the theatre is on its way out" (Devlin, 1986, 99; Lahr, 2014, 440–41). In his forthright *Memoirs*, in fact, he admitted that today's audiences seem "obdurately resistant to my kind of theatre. [… they] seem to be conditioned to a kind of theatre which is quite different from the kind I wish to practice. […] I am quite through with the kind of plays that established my early and popular reputation" (Williams, 1975, xvii).

He embraced and absorbed such theatrical change and sought to follow, for a time, but in his own way, as he continues:

I am doing a different thing, which is altogether my own, not influenced at all by other playwrights at home or abroad or by other schools of theatre. My thing is what it always was, to express my world and my experience of it in whatever forms seem suitable to the material. (Williams, 1975, xvii)

That is, Williams seemed both to lament the change that appeared to diminish his sort of theater and to embrace the work of new playwrights, "who are exploring the subtleties of human relations that haven't been explored." As he suggested in a 1962 interview, "It's something that drives me crazy with jealousy. I love it. While I'm in the theatre, I'm enthralled by it and I say, Oh, God, if I could write like that. If only I were twenty-five and just starting out, what these boys could have given me" (Devlin, 1986, 98).[30] He was, thus, an enthusiastic supporter of and was perhaps regenerated by the work of a new generation of experimental playwrights like Harold Pinter, Edward Albee and Samuel Beckett.

European productions, like Davies's *Cat on a Hot Tin Roof* (1989), which returned to Williams's original third act and so rejected the sort of tailoring to contemporary Broadway taste that Kazan's rewritten third act for the New York premiere represented, tended to emphasize aesthetic over more commercial values. Davies's rethinking "the whole style" of *Cat on a Hot Tin Roof* was, thus, of a piece with Peter Hall's *Orpheus Descending* (1989–91) and with Benedict Andrews's "updated" 2017 revival of the *Cat on a Hot Tin Roof* deemed "so courageous" because of its overt nudity.

In Italy, Elio De Capitani's productions of *Un tram che si chiama desiderio* (1995) and *Improvvisamente, l'estate scorsa* (2011) were staged in fresh, new, up-to-date translations by Masolino D'Amico. These directors appear to have tapped into the energy and freshness that Williams found in that new generation of playwrights he called "these boys." Contemporary European directors seem, somehow, to have recovered an innovative edge to Williams's theater blunted in so many American productions. Such a thread suggests the continued vitality of Williams's work in Europe, among directors willing to probe and rediscover his depths, to treat him as "a playwright worthy of further artistic investigation," as European audiences, correspondingly, seem less inclined to dismiss him as an artist whom history has overtaken.[31] But as many questions are raised as answered in such an assessment, as, for example, what actually constitutes innovation, the so-called rethinking "the whole style" of Williams? For De Capitani, much of it was generated linguistically with fresh translations replacing those made immediately or shortly after World War II. Rob Ashford's revival of *Cat on a Hot Tin Roof* at the Richard Rogers Theater in New York in 2013, with Scarlett Johansson, on the other hand, tended to rely on star power with which the producers had hoped to make the leap to London's West End: "There had been rumours that the sell-out [New York] production, directed by London-based Old Vic Associate Director Rob Ashford and which also stars Irish actor Ciaran Hands, would travel to the West End (Ashford directed [Rachel] Weisz in Williams' classic play *A Streetcar Named Desire* at the Donmar Warehouse in 2009)."[32] Too often, however, what passes for innovation, daring or rethinking means recalibrating the shock value of Williams's work, making more explicit what Williams left implicit, foregrounding elements the Lord Chamberlain found objectionable in the post–World War II British climate of the 40s and 50s; we have, then,

Benedict Andrews's 2017 nudity-laced version of *Cat on a Hot Tin Roof* produced by the Young Vic but which opened directly in the West End and was also subsequently broadcast internationally during the 2020 pandemic, although the obviously contrived southern accents of the cast, apparently used to punctuate the production's Southern American authenticity, wind up sounding risible if not painful, like warmed over *Dallas*.[33] Likewise, the feigned cunnilingus in Andrews's "radical overhaul" in his 2014 revival of *A Streetcar Named Desire* at the Young Vic, also streamed free worldwide to an international audience during the 2020 pandemic with the West End shut down, might be deemed unnecessary sensationalism even as the cast insisted, "We're not doing a full on sex show."[34] Whether such scenes are pandering or a legitimate probing of the work's depths remains as contentious as Williams's original rape scene in *A Streetcar Named Desire*. Williams himself had serious reservation about a coarsening of his work, particularly the language of *Cat on a Hot Tin Roof*: "I would regret very much if this new play had to rely even in a minor degree on the public's appetite for salaciousness. [...] when I heard that word was getting around that we had a dirty show filled with dirty dialogue I strongly advised their removal." Williams finally retained the coarseness of language since "it helped establish some of the characters, most of all the crude and uncouth Big Daddy" (Devlin, 1986, 34–35).

We might conclude, glibly perhaps, that the UK is still struggling with its legacy of sexual repression, driven especially by what Williams called the "intense honesty" of his plays, as, equally glibly, we might add that the United States remains entangled in the inextricable legacy of race, an issue that Williams tended to underplay in favor of other "outsider" and immigrant figures, although the Ku Klux Klan (called "the Mystic Crew") features directly in *Orpheus Descending*—and in other of his plays. That said, we can add that no comparable lineup of Williams's productions (or that of any other dramatist, American or not) can compete with those staged on the eastern side of the Atlantic, which observation returns us to, and perhaps revalidates, Rich's acute theatrical insight of 1988. Theater critic Gordon Rogoff put the matter even more bluntly as he opens his assessment of "Peter Hall's lucid passionate [London] production of *Orpheus* [*Descending*]" and in the process offers a coda to this broader reassessment of the arcs of Williams's professional reputation as the last word: "That the London West End is the home to what must be the best Tennessee Williams production in thirty years is only part of America's mounting national and theatrical disgrace. [...] Evidently, Broadway prefers death to the honor of going down fighting on behalf of a great American play acted with harrowing accuracy by a splendid cast" (Rogoff, 2000, 115).

Chapter 3

BECOMING SAMUEL BECKETT

TENNESSEE WILLIAMS AND THEATRICAL CHANGE ON THE POST–WORLD WAR II WORLD STAGE

I have only one major theme for my work, which is the destructive impact of society on the non-conformist individual.

—TW to agent Audrey Wood, in a letter of December 1939 from St. Louis

I have a distinct moralist attitude. I wouldn't say message. I'm not polemical, but I have a distinct attitude toward good and evil in life and people. I think any of my plays examined closely will indicate what I regard as evil. I think I regard hypocrisy and mendacity as almost the cardinal sins. It seems they are the ones to which I am most hostile. I think that deliberate, conscienceless mendacity, the acceptance of falsehood and hypocrisy, is the most dangerous of all sins.

—TW in conversation with William Burroughs, 1977

I am quite through with the kind of plays that established my early and popular reputation.

—TW, *Memoirs*, 1975

I think *Out Cry* is [...] influenced by Beckett.

—Ruby Cohn (Bray, 2002, 29)

Tennessee Williams may never have been the playwright we thought he was, or, at least, there has always been a Tennessee Williams we knew and understood (or thought we did) and a Williams we didn't. That division may be between early and late Williams, or between the Actors Studio Williams and a more poetical, lyrical Williams, or between, say, the Williams of *A Streetcar Named*

Desire and the Williams of *The Two-Character Play*. He was, it seems, always more lyrically Chekov than grittily Zola. His sin, if sin at all, was to have peaked too soon, as Gordon Rogoff reminds us, and thereby to have raised expectations in his audiences and among those handlers on whom theater relies, often strangers upon whose kindness Williams, too, depended (Rogoff, 2000, 59).

Opening a roundtable discussion on Williams's late plays in 2002,[1] however, Annette Saddik outlines a continuous thread between Williams's acknowledged successes and what we have come to think of as the later or lesser-known efforts:

> As early as *The Glass Menagerie*, he said in the production notes that realism wasn't really for him, that all it did was reproduce surfaces, and that he wanted to get to a distorted reality, an inner truth. And so, he's been called a poetic realist, but he never completely embraced that title. So in the later plays, where he completely abandoned realism, I think his goals remained the same. He wanted to articulate a truth, except his method had changed, in that he wasn't using the surfaces of reality any longer. He wasn't showing what reality looks like, but what reality is like beyond the surfaces. For example, in *The Two-Character Play*, or *Out Cry*, he wanted the setting to suggest a disordered mind rather than a specific place or time, as you can recognize in *A Streetcar Named Desire*, or *The Glass Menagerie*, or something of that nature. (Bray, 2002, 23)

Robert Bray, founding director of the Tennessee Williams Scholars Conference of which this roundtable was part, responds by suggesting that "with these later plays, we see the influence of certain playwrights, and his post-*Iguana* work has often been compared to the drama of Beckett, and Pinter, and Albee— occasionally in complimentary terms but more often to criticize Williams as a pale and unoriginal imitator" (Bray, 2002, 23–24; extended in Bray 2007, viii). Philip C. Kolin picks up the thread: "[…] in that late [*The Two-Character*] play, as he did in so many other late works, the theater itself became the subject of his inquiry. And, in that sense, it became very much a post-modern experience for him and for his audiences" (Bray, 2002, 24). Such a turn to theater as a subject might be deemed a turn *on* theater, a betrayal, something of a second sin, or, as Bray puts it, "Williams seems to be sometimes not only parodying theater but parodying his own work" (Bray, 2002, 25). In his introductory remarks, Bray cites Linda Dorff, who suggested that these later works constitute something of a "sub-genre." Bray will extend this critique of Dorff when he summarizes the 2002 roundtable panel in the introduction to his collection of such roundtables, *Tennessee Williams and His Contemporaries*, citing her description of the late plays as, "bawdy over the top farces that appropriate systems of metadrama and the aesthetics of cartoon to parody the stage [state?] of contemporary theater" (Bray, 2007, viii). Kolin would defend the metatheatrical nature of the late plays as follows: "What's on trial in Williams' [late] theater is the idea of theater itself" (Bray, 2002, 26). Saddik agrees, "the theater creates reality, it doesn't simply reflect it. And so, this focus on the theater as the subject of Williams' theater [is] his deconstruction of theater" (Bray, 2002, 26).

Much of this roundtable discussion with prominent Williams scholars recapitulates and extends what Williams himself has outlined in interviews and particularly in his forthright 1975 *Memoirs*. These he opens not with a discussion of *Streetcar* but with the vicissitudes of remaking himself as a playwright with, at first, a play called *Out Cry* that would finally develop through theatrical failure and subsequent rewritings into *The Two-Character Play*, "about which I will write from time to time in this book" (xv). The 1973 New Haven tryout included a parallel symposium at Yale University for what was billed as "an adventure in drama" and during which Williams felt as if he were at "an encampment of some failed war" (xvi).

One story he told the few Yale drama students in attendance was of a recent meeting with Gore Vidal, an old friend and, for a time, his traveling companion across Italy. As Williams described his enthusiasm about the dream cast for the impending production of *Out Cry*, Vidal responded, "Well Bird [Vidal's sobriquet for Williams], it won't do much good, I'm afraid, you've had too much bad personal exposure for anything to help you much anymore" (xvii). The inevitable question that followed from the audience was whether or not Vidal's assessment was an accurate appraisal of his theatrical reputation "here in the States" (xvii). Although he deflected the question during the symposium, its recollection prompts Williams in the *Memoirs* to muse: "The truth is I don't know whether or not I can ever again receive a persuasively favorable critical response to my theater work in this country," as audiences seem "obdurately resistant to my kind of theater these days" (xvii). Nevertheless, he retained hope, as he says of what became *The Two-Character Play* after the failure of *Out Cry*, "Ah, God. My life is hung on that production like a hat on a hook" (179).

And yet, despite a lack of immediate local American context, particularly of the mores of the American South, European artists and audiences may have related to him and his work, even or especially to the latter, more venturesome, more experimental Williams, and so accepted him more fully than American audiences have, at least with less disappointment. His continued, if not continuous, performance in European countries suggests a richer vitality than the playwright seems to enjoy in his native land, even in the earliest productions of *Streetcar* that were offered by well-known European and Central American theatrical artists: Seki Sano, often called "the father of Mexican theater," Luchino Visconti, Ingmar Bergman, Jean Cocteau and Laurence Olivier.

What is most often at issue has been that Tennessee Williams's later, experimental work ran counter to public and critical expectations established by his earlier achievements. The later plays seemed doomed to be compared to those earlier successes, and so they have often been problematic among critics, scholars, and audiences, as the playwright struggled to reinvent himself in a post-1960s cultural and theatrical climate that seems at times to have passed him by. What had been shocking frankness about desire and sexuality in 1947 with *Streetcar* became matter of fact in the Aquarian age of the tribal love musical *Hair* (1967) and the recreational sex romp *Oh! Calcutta!* (1969). Both Williams and Samuel Beckett contributed to the latter, Beckett unwittingly and even as Williams's sketch was rejected and cut before opening night.

Williams's decline, as Bray suggests, is often marked with those plays following 1961's *The Night of the Iguana*, which was generally praised, but, to Williams's dismay, the work did not receive a national tour.[2] *The Milk Train Doesn't Stop Here Anymore* of January 1963, on the other hand, was subject to substantial critical ridicule.[3] This post-1961 period of creative decline paralleled a series of substantial physical and emotional crises in Williams's life, including the death from lung cancer of his long-time companion, Frank Merlo, in 1961, which led to nearly a decade-long depression and years of psychoanalysis culminating in a nervous breakdown in 1969. However, the period saw Williams produce a series of deeply autobiographical works as well, plays precisely detailing that decline which deserve critical reappraisal and major theatrical revivals. He absorbed much of this cultural and theatrical change and sought to embrace it, for a time, in his own way:

> I am doing a different thing, which is altogether my own, not influenced at all by other playwrights at home or abroad or by other schools of theatre. My thing is what it always was, to express my world and my experience of it in whatever forms seems suitable to the material. (Williams, 1975, vxii)[4]

Chief among these is the one he considered the best of this denigrated period, a work called for a time and first performed as *Out Cry*, that is, *cri de coeur*, and then finally as *The Two-Character Play*: "It's a history of what I went through in the Sixties transmuted into the predicament of a brother and a sister" (Devlin, 1986, 239).

The late 1950s and 1960s, then, were not kind to Williams, personally and professionally. On the one hand, as some critics carped, his plays were always dark, "plunging into the sewers," as Los Angeles gossip columnist Hedda Hopper put it. He took the charge seriously and responded in November of 1958 by writing what he called "a serious comedy," appropriately named *Period of Adjustment*, a less-than-dark look at a pair of dysfunctional married couples in the wake of the Korean War. The play was previewed at the Coconut Grove Theater in Miami, Florida, on December 29, 1959, these early tryouts directed by Williams himself, before its opening at the Helen Hayes Theater, directed by George Roy Hill, nearly a year later, on November 10, 1960. It ran in New York for a respectable, if unspectacular, 132 performances, closing on March 4, 1961. Despite the attempt at comedy, the play returned to what had become some of Williams's central themes. It explored what today we would call post-traumatic stress disorder, including feelings of inadequacy in the elder of the two males, but the work ends, finally, with adjustment (hence the title) and reconciliation.

A film version that opened in 1962, called by promoters "Tennessee Williams's Great First Comedy," was co-written by Williams. Its release coincided with the publication of the text as a Signet book, a cheap, 50-cent, mass-market paperback that all but forced comparisons to Williams's earlier work: the cover announced, "Tennessee Williams: author of *Cat on a Hot Tin Roof*," and the back cover read, "From scorching drama to *saucy* comedy" and "his hilarious, *uninhibited comedy* about husbands, wives, and honeymoons." The blurb on the front cover further raised expectations: "The Pulitzer Prize-winning author's *uninhibited comedy* about the oldest games of the sexes—marital dares. Now a *saucy* M. G. M. motion picture release starring Tony Franciosa, Jane Fonda, Tim Hutton" (emphases added).

However, a shift of tone toward comedy seemed not to be the solution to the issues Williams faced with critics, audiences, and, finally, with himself. He defended his work and his darker themes in the *New York Times* on the eve of the Broadway opening of *Period of Adjustment*: "The theatre has made its greatest artistic advances through the unlocking and lighting up and ventilation of closets, attics and basements of human behavior and experience. No significant area of human experience should be inaccessible, provided it is presented with honest intention and taste, to the writers of our desperate time." It is a position he will attribute to Ernest Hemingway in one of his least-admired late plays, *Clothes for a Summer Hotel*.

That is, while Williams searched and struggled for new subjects and to develop a new theatrical voice in the 1960s, he seemed to return continually to his lifelong preoccupations. *Clothes for a Summer Hotel: A Ghost Play* is one such meditation, a very personal self-examination that is often seen as another attempt to confront and come to grips with the mental issues that dominated his sister Rose's life. These issues, explored through the character of Zelda Fitzgerald, whose creativity and sexuality had been constrained, Williams thought were endemic to his family, and would eventually affect him as well. Yet even with such thematic consistency, *Clothes for a Summer Hotel* represented something of a major departure for Williams, since it took as its subject the relationship between novelist F. Scott Fitzgerald and his wife Zelda, a couple Williams never met. The play is set at a point long after Zelda was institutionalized in the Highland Mental Hospital in Asheville, North Carolina. Her novelist husband was in poor health, plagued with alcoholism and in creative decline himself but on the verge of a late breakthrough novel, *The Love of the Last Tycoon*. The novel was never completed, but it was published as *The Last Tycoon*, edited by Edmund Wilson, in 1941, and, finally, under Fitzgerald's original title, *The Love of the Last Tycoon*, edited from Fitzgerald's notes by Matthew J. Bruccoli, in 1993. *Clothes* would be Williams's last Broadway play. It opened on March 26, 1980, directed by an ailing José Quintero, who, Williams thought, could not give his full attention to the play.[5] With Geraldine Page as Zelda and Kenneth Haigh as Scott Fitzgerald, the play previewed at the Eisenhower Theater at the Kennedy Center in Washington, DC. There it ran between January 28 and February 23, to devastating reviews that sent Williams into a mad rush of rewriting. It moved next to Chicago in late February for further previews, but fared no better. *Clothes* opened subsequently and, as it turned out, again inauspiciously at the Cort Theatre in New York, amid a heavy springtime blizzard and a concurrent strike of the city's transit workers. The city was all but paralyzed. The play ran on Broadway for just fifteen performances. Writing in the *New York Times* on March 27, 1980, Walter Kerr lamented that

> Mr. Williams' personal voice is nowhere to be heard in it. It is as though the playwright's decision to deal with actual people—not only the Fitzgeralds but Ernest Hemingway and the Gerald Murphys as well— had momentarily robbed him of his own imaginative powers. [...] no one is able to do a single thing to bring the performances to plausible, troubled, passionate life. ("The Home" section, D 16)

John Beaufort, writing in the *Christian Science Monitor* on March 27, 1980, concluded his usually sympathetic review as follows: "One cannot help wondering whether this plunge into a ghostly purgatory was worth all the trouble it has taken." The play has been rarely revived since and inauspiciously so when it has been attempted.

Other critics attacked what they saw as factual inaccuracy in the historical lives of the principal characters, Scott and Zelda, even as Williams took pains to remind his audience and readers frequently of the work's experimental and lyrical qualities. He stressed these in a program note in 1980, then again on publication of the revised text by New Directions in 1983. In the stage directions themselves Williams wrote:

> This must be regarded as a ghost play because of the chronological licenses which are taken, comparable to those we have taken in *Camino Real*, the purpose being to penetrate into character more deeply and to encompass dreamlike passages of time in a scene.

Again in the "Author's Note: This is a ghost play":

> Of course, in a sense, all plays are ghost plays, since players are not actually whom they play.

> Our reason for taking extraordinary license with time and place is that in an asylum and on its grounds liberties of this kind are quite prevalent: and also these liberties allow us to explore in more depth what we believe is truth in character.

As Zelda says in the first scene, "the mind of a lunatic is not—retentive of present things" (8). And the play is set after the deaths of all the principles, as Zelda informs us, "I thought that obligations stopped with death" (8). Moreover, the play is less about the Fitzgeralds than about the Williamses, as producer Elliot Martin insisted after the play's New York closing:

> It's not about the Fitzgeralds, it's about a brother and sister, about Tennessee and his sister, with the image of the asylum looming over all. And it's a play with a certain transferred paranoia—from the situation of Rose to that of Williams himself who [exactly like the tortured and alcoholic F. Scott Fitzgerald] was blaming the critics and the media for his own failures. (Spoto, 1985, 345)

Writing of a revival of the play at the Hudson Guild Theater in New York's Chelsea district on February 2, 2010, Dan Callahan focused on what he saw as one of the play's digressions. It is, in fact, a scene that reintroduces and develops critical issues surrounding Williams's sexuality. Callahan notes that Williams

> stops his play cold for an excruciating exchange between Fitzgerald and his rival pal Ernest Hemingway where the two writers keep talking about their own femininity as revealed in their various short stories; it's one of

the worst scenes Williams ever wrote, a meandering, half-bored sniffing out of the repressed gay leanings of the two most famous American novelists of the twenties and thirties.

In reality, the scene was one that Williams worked on with some diligence and deliberation and expanded for the work's 1983 publication. Williams has been quite clear about the purpose of the expanded scene even as he had to cut an hour from the original production: "Hemingway had a remarkable interest in and understanding of homosexuality, for a man who was not a homosexual. I think both Hemingway and Fitzgerald had elements of homosexuality in them" (Devlin, 1986, 347). Williams goes on to cite the Hemingway short story "A Simple Inquiry" and the ending to *Islands in the Stream*, the former an apparent solicitation, the latter a love declaration between men. While Walter Kerr's review was characteristic of the reception that *Clothes for a Summer Hotel* received in its original performance, few critics have recognized that much of Williams's "personal voice" and the seat of much of his "imaginative powers" remain in this play, in his exploration of sexuality, especially repressed sexuality, and more often than not through the sensitive depiction of oppressed female characters. As he said in a notebook entry of September 26, 1943, "My world is a world of a few ideas and a few simple feelings to which I try to be faithful" (Williams, 2006, 385).

In the aftermath of Williams's sudden, accidental and unexpected death in 1983, Gore Vidal focused on Williams's depiction of women: "There is no actress on earth who will not testify that Williams created the best women characters in the modern theatre." Writing in *Edge Boston* on the occasion of the Williams centenary in 2011, Robert Israel noted: "You need only look at the names of the actresses (living and dead) who received accolades for playing Williams' heroines: Laurette Taylor, Jessica Tandy, Vivien Leigh, Geraldine Page, Katherine Hepburn, Maureen Stapleton, Gertrude Lawrence, Bette Davis, Tallulah Bankhead, Elizabeth Ashley, Anna Magnani, Kim Stanley, Kathleen Turner and, of course, the late Elizabeth Taylor." Vidal went on in his assessment of Williams to tie this depiction of women to Williams's own sexuality: "It is widely believed that since Tennessee Williams liked to have sex with men (true), he hated women (untrue); as a result his women characters are thought to be malicious creatures, designed to subvert and destroy godly straightness."[6]

The issue that Vidal was addressing, the critical assault on the interlaced themes of Williams's personal sexuality and his depiction of women, began in the 1960s. Howard Taubman, drama critic of the *New York Times*, fired the first volley, accusing Williams of portraying women as destroyers and sex maniacs. They were, said Taubman, homosexuals in disguise. Six years later, the paper's new drama critic, Stanley Kauffmann, was still castigating Williams's "viciousness towards women, the lurid violence [...] (and) the transvestite sexual exhibitionism." On June 15, 1995, the eve of its British revival, David Benedict took on the still-lingering issue of Williams's women directly. The play was *Sweet Bird of Youth*, whose principal female character, Alexandra Del Lago, traveling under the name of Princess Kosmonopolis (and played by Geraldine Page in the 1959 Broadway opening), seems something of a predatory female. Benedict writes: "That they are merely feminised men has been disproved time and again. Unlike critics, actresses are never surprised by his admission that 'I have had many close relationships with men which were without any sexual connotations, God knows. But I have found them less deeply satisfying than those I have had with a few women.'"

From such a perspective, then, the central figure and topic of *Clothes for a Summer Hotel* is Zelda and her sexuality, not Scott and his. Paraphrasing Williams in 1979, John Hicks noted that "he feels akin to Zelda, burned to death in a North Carolina asylum fire in 1948, eight years after her husband died" (Devlin, 1986, 321). Zelda then was another of Williams's Southern belles who had an affair, in Zelda's case in 1926 in the south of France with a French aviator, Edouard (who also doubles as an Intern in the asylum, the Highland Hospital). Their relationship Williams saw as "the first time she was experiencing erotic ecstasy" (Devlin, 1986, 359). Scott in this love triangle, then, is sexually inadequate, a self-doubt which is much of the point of the disparaged Fitzgerald/Hemingway scene. Such "erotic ecstasy" was featured on the play's publicity so that the play's passion is associated with the "flaming bush" at the asylum and the fire that will eventually kill her, trapped as she was within the locked asylum. After a series of violent outbursts with the aviator, however, Zelda attempts suicide as her affair with Edouard is ending in act 2. "I did this in honor of my love for you," she tells him at the Murphys' party, "I swallowed all the contents of a bottle of narcotics!" (50). That is, Zelda is caught between desire and the cultural pressure that stifles women's passions and creativity. Her lover Edouard notes at the opening of act 2: "I heard loud voices downstairs—while you were crying out so wildly during your—" (42).

On the imaginary visit with which the play opens, Scott has flown out from Los Angeles amid reports of serious changes in Zelda's condition, which he claims the doctors called her "remarkable improvement" (9). He is in North Carolina, thus, for a perfunctory visit, just for the day, and so is dressed inappropriately, as Zelda reminds him, "as if about to check in at a summer hotel" (9). The reunion is strained from the first, held outside the Gothic asylum in the howling wind. Zelda, dressed in a tutu, has continued to study classical ballet: "The career that I undertook because you forbade me to write. […] No, I respect your priority in the career of writing although it proceeded to eclipse my own. I made a sacrifice to you and so elected ballet" (13–14). Of course, she is much too old for the rigorous training of classical ballet, as she recounts in a hallucination of the years in Paris, "Mme. Egorova feels I've embarked upon a dance career rather late in life, but she says that with such application and such longing, such dedication, I can make up for delay" (19). With her gift of Cassandra, Zelda has a premonition: "I WILL DIE IN FLAMES!" (15).

Scene 2 picks up Scott at work in 1926 but drinking heavily, and the conversation turns to Scott's "prettiness," which he takes as an assault on his virility as Zelda mentions the men who seem attracted to him. "I think that to write well about women," she notes, "there's got to be that [female or gay trait], a part of that, oh, not too much, not so much that he flits about like a…." Scott finishes her phrase, "Fairy?" (31). Zelda is prompted in this conversation by an event at the beach in which a stranger shows her a copy of a magazine from Scott's university days, *The Princeton Triangle Club*, in which Scott cross-dressed for a theatrical event. "Somebody had to appear as the ingénue in it.—That year I was chosen to play it. Yes, that's me. What of it" (33). A second scene within scene 2 finds Zelda on the beach of the *Côte Azure* with Edouard, who restricts her public show of affection and so constrains her passions. Zelda calls him "a gentleman flyer so attached to convention" (47). With scene 2, then, Zelda is frustrated by both men in her life, albeit for slightly different reasons. She arranges a *rendezvous* with Edouard at a discrete *Auberge Rêve Bleu*, where act 2 will commence.

Act 2 opens with Edouard and Zelda in a "*chambre*," "*nude except for whatever conventions of stage propriety may be in order*" (41), as the stage directions suggest. Scott, having discerned the tryst, sits outside the *Auberge*. He is the famed author, but the poetry in the play belongs to Zelda, who had earlier called herself Daisy, and so recreated the Fitzgerald character from *The Great Gatsby*. "If he makes me a monument with his carefully arranged words, is that my life, my recompense for madness?" (44). Zelda's passion is as frightening to her discrete male lover as it is to her husband. To Edouard she boasts, "I'd be quite willing to perform the act of love with you at the height of a cloudless noon, on top of the *Arc de triomphe*, enormously magnified for all of Paris, all the *world* to see" (49), but both the men in her life seem to be telling her, "*Don't live!*" (50). Scott abandons his work and arrives at the Murphys' dance with word of Joseph Conrad's death. "We've lost our only writer with a true tragic sense" (52), he announces to the indifferent guests. As the scenes fluidly move from the south of France back to the Asheville asylum, Scott confronts Zelda's doctor, Zeller, whom he confuses with one from Zelda's Swiss sanitarium. Zeller tells him about Zelda's creative work: "I like to read important writing,

Figure 3.1 José Quintero's pre-Broadway tryout of *Clothes for a Summer Hotel* at The Kennedy Center, DC, January 1980. Poster features the passion of Zelda

and I feel that your wife's novel *Save Me the Waltz*—I'm sure you won't mind my saying that there are passages in it that have a lyrical imagery that moves me, sometimes, more that your own. [...]—I'm sorry to say this to you, but I never quite found anything in yours, even yours, equal to it" (55).

The scene shifts back to the Murphys' party as the Hemingways arrive, which leads to the homoerotic exchange between Scott and "Hem." Hemingway notes, "It is said that the duality of gender can serve some writers well" (64), as he and Scott exchange reminiscences of a "tender night" in Lyon. Hemingway's defense is professional: "it's my profession to observe and interpret all kinds of human relations" (65), a response that suggests Williams speaking in his own voice. Hemingway makes clear that the audience is listening to ghosts, all the principals long dead: "We sang that song together the night before I chose to blast my brains out for no reason but the good and sufficient reason that my work was finished. [...] No reason for me to continue" (68).

But the final scene belongs to Zelda. *Clothes for a Summer Hotel* is her play, and she is at her most poetic in the last scene, the farewell to Scott beside the "flaming bush" where the play opened. Here she has the air both of Blanche Dubois—"The last time I was home with Mother in Montgomery [Alabama] I used to ride the trolley car to the end of the line" (71) —as well as of Scott—"A delightful surprise to find myself remembered by an old beau" (76). It is she who has the final triumph of self-understanding denied her male counterparts, as she notes in her final lines, "I'm not your book! Anymore!" She tells Scott, "*I can't be your book anymore! Write yourself a new book!*" (77).

Hemingway will indeed "blast his brains out" (or has); Scott will succumb (has succumbed) to his heart condition; Zelda will perish in the asylum fire (well before this ghost play commenced). It is among the most touching endings in all of Williams, as tender as the night, with a heroine both strong and vulnerable, whose triumph is her refusal to live illusions or honor conventions. It is an almost unknown Williams play, both thematically consistent and radically new and fresh, a play that cries out for revival and translation.

Among other experimental plays, *In the Bar of a Tokyo Hotel* opened off-Broadway in 1969. Critic Clive Barnes could write in the *New York Times* that the play finally "repelled" him, as he lamented that it "seems almost too personal, and as a result too painful, to be seen in the cold light of public scrutiny. Mr. Williams has, perhaps, never been overreluctant to show the world his wounds—but in his new play he seems to be doing nothing else." Barnes denigrates it finally as "Mr. Williams' sad bird of loneliness." But the sagacious Barnes also saw experimental touches in the play, noting that "there are more flashes of genius here than in any of his later plays," the playwright struggling to find a new voice, a new theater, even, as the play's central character, a dying painter named Mark, struggles (like his author) to find a new mode of expression. When "the actor who plays [Mark] confronts the audience and, with an almost Pirandellian shift of key, says calmly: 'I was talking to myself,' it is neither actor nor painter we can think of, but Williams himself" (May 12, 1969). One might have hoped for something like a successful revival of this play in or near the centenary year of 2011, a resurgence of interest in Williams's late works in a new age more sympathetic to artistic experiment, but the most recent revival, with its attempt at updating with a techno-restructuring, was disastrous. *In the Bar of a Tokyo Hotel* opened off-Broadway, at the New World Stages theater complex in Midtown Manhattan at 340 West 50th Street, on October 17, 2012, directed and choreographed by Maria Torres ("creative director"), complete with three-dimensional projections to accompany the choreography. The play fared even worse with critics and audiences than earlier productions and did little more than further damage Williams's reputation. *New York Post* critic Elisabeth Vincentelli, in something of an anti-review, entitled "Wretched 'In the Bar of a Tokyo Hotel' adds insult to injury," called it "amateurishly ghastly" and "a sad, sad mess." It certainly didn't help that the original lead actress, Reiko Aylesworth, abandoned the show before opening night. It closed on October 28.

Williams acknowledged that attitudes towards sexuality changed drastically in his creative lifetime, as well as that theater itself was moving in new directions. He could be enthusiastic about such changes in the theater and supported the work of what he called "this new wave of playwrights."

***

In their entry on Samuel Beckett in the *Critical Companion to Tennessee Williams*, Greta Heintzelman and Alycia Smith-Howard remark, almost offhandedly, that "Williams admired the work of Beckett and was instrumental in introducing him to U. S. audiences." They cite his late plays as his attempt to work in something of a Beckettian mode, including *In the Bar of a Tokyo Hotel* and the play published and performed under the titles *Out Cry* and *The Two-Character Play*. Heintzelman and Smith-Howard offer neither arguments nor supporting details for their short encyclopedia entry. We do know, however, that Williams may have read *Waiting for Godot* as early as 1957 when the complete, if curiously jumbled, nearly incoherent text appeared in the April 1956 issue of *Theatre Arts* magazine (36–61). The journal also carried a story about an early tryout production of *Sweet Bird of Youth* (which some critics consider Williams's last great play) at Studio M Playhouse (66–67), a community theater in Miami, Florida. This was not far from where *Waiting for Godot* had its ill-fated American premiere at the Coconut Grove Playhouse in January of 1955, two years to the day after its Paris world premiere. Williams might also have read the first American edition of *Godot* published by Grove Press, available as early as 1954, before the Miami and New York productions. Alternately, he may have seen and/or read the (censored) British edition published by Faber and Faber the following year to coincide with the London premiere at the Arts Theatre on August 3, 1955, since he called *Godot* director Peter Hall shortly after *Godot* opened in London to ask if Hall were interested in staging his own work. In any case, he surely would have seen and read the curiously scrambled text of *Godot* by April of 1956 in the issue of *Theatre Arts* magazine that contained both the full text of *Waiting for Godot* and the story about the Miami performance of *Sweet Bird of Youth*. If nothing else, the juxtaposition suggests a changing theatrical era. Williams was, in fact, already somewhat defensive about the opening of *Sweet Bird of Youth*, since, to his mind, its tryout production was still an untested and unrevised version of the play. Williams noted "the extremely short interval between the writing and production, and he called the play 'a work in progress—one which had been undergoing continual change up to and including actual rehearsal'" (Williams, 1956, 67).

Alan Levy, in his essay on the history of *Godot* in the same issue of *Theater Arts*, "The Long Wait for Godot," concluded his piece by affirming that

> *Waiting for Godot* has been 'adopted' by three Pulitzer Prize playwrights—
> Tennessee Williams, Thorton Wilder, [who spent considerable time
> rewriting *Godot*, which version American director Alan Schneider used
> substantially for his Miami staging], and William Saroyan [who would
> write the lukewarm liner notes for the CBS recording of the New York
> production]. Williams regards *Godot* as one of the greatest plays of
> modern times and invested in [Michael] Myerberg's productions. (Levy,
> 1956, 96)

Presumably, the plural suggests both Miami and, perhaps, two New York productions, the second an African American *Godot*.

Although his decline is frequently dated from the 1960s, by the end of the 1950s Williams was already struggling. His rewriting of the Orpheus myth into *Orpheus Descending*, itself a recasting of *Battle of Angels* that had closed in its Boston tryout in 1940, opened on Broadway on March 21, 1957, and Williams was already moving to another sort of drama. As critic Charles A. Goldthwaite Jr. has noted, "the play is clearly in dialogue with Norman Mailer's 1957 essay 'The White Negro,' an imperfect but influential expression of contemporary white male perceptions of African-American masculinity." But *Orpheus* ran for just 68 performances on Broadway.[7] Even with a successful British revival, critic Michael Kuchwara, writing for the Associated Press, is reluctant to praise play and playwright: "Peter Hall's production of *Orpheus Descending* by Tennessee Williams is a first-rate revival of a second-rate play." He further notes that the stars of the production are the actress and director: "Miss Redgrave is often riveting, but the real hero of the evening is Hall who directs Williams' overwritten, overwrought and oversexed fandango with the commitment of a true believer" (Kuchwara). On the other hand, Gordon Rogoff saw Hall's American, if not Americanized, migration of his London production, now with a dominantly American cast (required by Actors' Equity), as a decided falling off:

> Peter Hall has turned his London production of *Orpheus Descending*—
> its grandeur sinister and stealthily appalled—into a less startled, more
> emphatic, noisy cartoon [cf. Druff above]. What was once weighted
> and balanced to present tarnished innocence colliding with amiable
> brutality now leans heavily on the brutal side, sound levels are up in
> Stephen Edward's electronic score, some of the women's costumes are
> in more garish colors, and Val Xavier [the Elvis Presley figure] has been

transformed from willow to oak, not noticeably different in spirit or voice from the redneck monsters pursuing his skin. (Rogoff, 2000, 117–18)

Frank Rich, who also had seen both London and New York productions, is more sanguine, as he extols Vanessa Redgrave's performance as she carries

the grotesque fate that Williams holds in store for his lovers thereafter, and that brings Miss Redgrave's performance to its devastating, tragic peak, is the substance not only of 'Orpheus Descending' but of the playwright's life work as well. Lady and Val are sensitive nonconformists who, like that sweet bird and like most Williams protagonists, must be destroyed by the bullying real world as soon as they come down to earth. A two-month flop when staged by Harold Clurman[8] on Broadway in 1957, 'Orpheus Descending' can now be seen as a pivotal chapter in the author's canon, reverberating throughout his career. [...] In 1957, "Orpheus" was the boundary between Williams' biggest successes and saddest theatrical travails. (Rich, 1988)

But while Rich remains in thrall of Redgrave, Hall, and this iteration of Williams, he shares Rogoff's disappointment with the replacement of the British actors with American ones: "One would expect American actors to do better by Williams than their London counterparts, but whether through miscasting or underrehearsing, that's not the case here." Rich can be as devastating as Rogoff: "As a result, this 'Orpheus' is more of a triumph for Miss Redgrave than for Williams, whose script reveals its seams when in the other actors' hands. But since everything the star does is in the playwright's service, his spirit always comes through, even when passages of his play do not" (Rich, 1988).

Much of what some might deem as neglect of Williams's work in the United States, or his confinement by the expectations of previous successes, has indeed constituted something of a falling off, fueled, perhaps, also by a preoccupation if not obsession with his tempestuous life that too often overshadowed his work. Except for the enthusiastic reception of Williams's first two plays in European countries, A Streetcar Named Desire having premiered in most major European capitals by 1949, Williams was embraced most fully in Europe only after his death, something of the reverse of the American pattern. Hall's production of Orpheus is a case in point, at least in its London iteration.

Yet even as Williams would begin to lose favor in his own country, major Italian initiatives of his work continued. In 1991, with Williams's reputation in the States at its ebb, the Festival dei Due Mondi di Spoleto and the Teatro Nuovo di Milano commissioned a new translation of the standard postwar

"Not merely Miss Redgrave's personal triumph. It is a landmark production full of implications for the American theatre."
—Frank Rich, The New York Times

Figure 3.2 Peter Hall's 1989 revival of *Orpheus Descending* in New York

version of the play by Gerardo Guerrieri, the theater critic for *La Stampa*. The new performance version was by Masolino D'Amico, professor of English literature at Università degli studi Roma Tre. Under the direction of Elio De Capitani, who began his theatrical career with the Teatro dell'Elfo in 1973, the production opened at the Teatro San Nicolò di Spoleto on July 2, 1993, with Aleksander Cvjetkovic as Stanley, Mariangela Melato as Blanche, and Ester Galazzi as Stella, with Giancarlo Previati as Mitch. It went on to play at the Teatro Eliseo and Teatro di Genova, among others. Furthermore, in the centenary year of 2011, where Williams was conspicuously missing from Broadway, De Capitani returned to his passion, as he says in the program note to *Improvvisamente, l'estate scorsa* [*Suddenly, Last Summer*]. Teaming up with translator Masolino D'Amico once again, *Improvvisamente, l'estate scorsa* opened at Elfo Puccini in Milan on May 3, 2011, with Cristina Crippa as the bird-like Mrs. Venable and Elena Russo Arman as her adversary, Catherine Holly. Cristian Giammarini played Dr. Curkowicz. It was a brave choice by De Capitani, since the long one-act play was only half of the program that opened in New York in January of 1958 under the collective title *The Garden District* (a neighborhood of New Orleans). The second half, *Something Unspoken*,

Figure 3.3 Elio De Capitani's Milan revival of *Improvvisamente, l'estate scorsa* [*Suddenly, Last Summer*], 2011

was dismissed as "a trifling, inconclusive anecdote" (Atkinson) and so has had little life beyond its initial coupling with *Suddenly, Last Summer* (although both were revived on October 16, 1995, at the famed Circle in the Square theater in New York). The 1959 film version of *Suddenly, Last Summer*, on the other hand, in Gore Vidal's adaptation of the play with its famous asylum scene, turned Elizabeth Taylor into a sex symbol as the asylum's inmates respond to her presence, a raw sexuality that made explicit her role as Sebastian's procurer on the Mexican beach in her equally famous "transparent" bathing suit. De Capitani's stage production remains in the lush, tropical, semi-surrealistic garden of Mrs. Venable's antebellum house in New Orleans's Garden District, complete with huge, flesh-eating plants, without the film's spectacular reenactments. It is here, in the ostentation of the garden, that the aging, wealthy, protective dowager exercises her wealth and will to control her son's legacy by plotting to have her niece, Sebastian's companion on that fateful summer's day, lobotomized, and thereby to put an end to Catherine's tales of procurement, homosexuality, and cannibalism that seemed to mark his end, suddenly,[9] last summer. Brooks Atkinson was curiously ambivalent about the original 1958 production, praising its use of language but finally deeming the world of Williams "infected" and "corrupt":

At this late date it is no longer necessary to observe that Tennessee Williams is a writer.

But one of his two short plays, put on last evening at the York Playhouse (First Avenue and Sixty-fourth Street), is startling proof of what a man can do with words. It is called "Suddenly, Last Summer," the second of the plays produced under the group title of "Garden District"; and you can be sure that it has horrifying things to say. Mr. Williams is not the man to dismiss anyone from the theatre without shocking everyone's sensibilities.

Nor is he the man to use words carelessly. "Suddenly, Last Summer" is an exercise in the necromancy of writing. Out of words set down with lyrical facility, Mr. Williams constructs an infected world. [...]

"Suddenly, Last Summer" is further evidence of Mr. Williams' genius with the language. Although his world is tainted with corruption, it is beautifully contrived. No one else can use ordinary words with so much grace, allusiveness, sorcery and power. (Atkinson)

De Capitani's hyperrealistic set complete with shrieking bird calls is a far cry from the stark, symbolic production of Memorie Futuro under the direction of Danilo Canzanella, which appeared at Rome's Teatro Albertino in February 2010. There George Holly, Catherine's brother, reappears at the end as a symbolic Christ, even perhaps as an image or reincarnation of Sebastian as well. De Capitani's production indulges in no such excess, and refrains from depicting "an infected world," but in the text and production Mrs. Venable is fully ambulatory except for the cane she wields, and Doctor Curkowicz, who is romantically involved with Catherine here, signs the papers authorizing her lobotomy even as he notes, in the last lines of the Williams text, "I think we ought to at least consider the possibility that the girl's story could be true" (*Suddenly* 93). Nonetheless, De Capitani's gripping and deeply psychological probing of this infrequently performed Williams text suggests the continued active engagement between the work of Tennessee Williams and that of Italian theater directors.

In 2012, Capitani returned to another maligned Williams work and staged its Italian premiere at *Spoleto55 Festival dei 2Mondi* [*sic*] in July of 2012, moving it to Milan's Elfo Puccini in October of that year. The website for Elfo Puccini surveys the play's uncertain history:

La discesa di Orfeo (rielaborazione di un'opera composta da Williams nel 1940, *Battle of Angels*, che morì sul nascere) fu rappresentato per la

prima volta nel marzo del 1957 a New York. Gli interpreti principali—
Maureeen Stapleton e Cliff Robertson—vennero ben accolti dalla
critica, ma lo spettacolo ebbe poca fortuna, restando in scena solo due
mesi. Maggiore successo ebbe la trasposizione per il grande schermo che
Sidney Lumet realizzò poco dopo, con il titolo *The fugitive kind* (in italiano
Pelle di serpente) e con protagonisti Anna Magnani e Marlon Brando.
Bisogna aspettare il 1988 per rivedere un allestimento importante,
capace di riaccendere i riflettori su questo ancora semisconosciuto;
Peter Hall lo scelse per la produzione inaugurale della sua Peter Hall
Company, portandolo al successo, tanto che Frank Rich sul *New York
Times*, giudicò lo spettacolo "una pietra miliare". Nel 1990 Peter Hall ne
girò anche una versione cinematografica fedele la sua regia teatrale, con
Vanessa Redgrave, Kevin Anderson e il resto del cast che aveva trionfato
a Londra e a Broadway l'anno prima.

Orpheus Descending (a reworking of a work by Williams in 1940, *Battle of
Angels*, which closed in its Boston tryouts) was first presented in March
of 1957 in New York. The principal performers—Maureeen Stapleton
and Cliff Robertson—were well received by critics, but the play ran for
only two months. It had more success on the big screen in a version
that Sidney Lumet directed shortly thereafter under the title *The Fugitive
Kind* (*Pelle di serpente* in Italian) with Anna Magnani and Marlon Brando.
We have had to wait until 1988 to see an important stage performance
highlighting this still little-known work. Peter Hall chose *Orpheus Descending*
for the inaugural production of his Peter Hall Company, which brought
him immediate success [see above]. Writing in the *The New York Times*
Frank Rich declared it "a milestone." In 1990 Hall also filmed a faithful
version of his theatrical staging with Vanessa Redgrave, Kevin Anderson
and the rest of the cast that had triumphed in London and Broadway
the previous year. [My translation.]

In June of 2013, yet another of the much-maligned late plays, and, for some,
the best of them, opened in the same theater where *In the Bar of a Tokyo Hotel*
had failed so miserably the preceding September. Writing in the *New York Times*
on June 21, 2013, senior *Times* critic Ben Brantley in a review called "Brother,
Can You Spare My Sanity? Amanda Plummer and Brad Dourif in Tennessee
Williams Rarity" suggests something of a turnaround for the reputation of
Williams's late plays. The "rarity" was *The Two-Character Play*. Williams called
it "a play within a play within a play," his "most beautiful play since *Streetcar*"
(Devlin, 239), and "my best play since *Cat* [...] Maybe better" (Devlin, 164).[10]
"Produced by David Merrick in 1973 on Broadway," Brantley notes,

it ran for 12 performances under its original title, "Out Cry." Though critics were mostly respectful, if baffled, you can understand why it failed. It's low on plot and high on poetry, and it presents the painful spectacle of a talented, desperate mind chasing itself in circles. It probably didn't help that the stars of "Out Cry" were the young and beautiful Michael York and Cara Duff-MacCormick.

The cast of the Plummer and Dourif Production, according to Brantley, do not share the character defects of youth and beauty. Like *Orpheus* in 1989, it again seems to have taken a European director to breathe life into this American play. Gene David Kirk, artistic director of London's Jermyn Street Theatre, staged it in London in 2010, brought it to the Provincetown Tennessee Williams Theater Festival the following September, and, with a new and now stellar American cast, brought it to off-Broadway in the summer of 2013. It was also Kirk who directed the world premiere of Williams's 1980 play *A Cavalier for Milady* at the Cock Tavern in 2011. Of Williams's late-career creative decline, Kirk notes:

> I don't think there was an aesthetic decline. There was an aesthetic change, that people then imposed their narrative of decline upon. What I think he was doing when he wrote something like *The Two-Character Play*, which I directed last year, people couldn't cope with it because it wasn't *Streetcar* or *Cat*, it didn't have this Williams naturalism if you like. *Glass Menagerie* deals with some of those in-and-out-of-time moments, which *Two-Character Play* does so much more, but it was as though it was from a different pen, even though the themes were the same. [...] Now when you consider, the critical success of a small theatre in London had last year with *The Two-Character Play* it took a Brit to kind of take it on and make it work. Which is bizarre. So now we're going to Provincetown as the centrepiece of the Tennessee Williams Festival there, then onto New Haven, and I'm currently talking to an off-Broadway producer about putting it on there. Now this is the play that suffered massively in the 70s, so "Un-Williams" and too complicated, now it's like "Oh my goodness. We've missed it" [...] you need a distance from the work in order to appreciate it. (Yates, 2011)

Kirk would be responsible for the staging of Samuel Beckett's radio play *All That Fall*, starring Eileen Atkins and Michael Gambon and directed by Trevor Nunn. Before he severed ties completely with the Off-West End Jermyn Street Theatre, Kirk scheduled Robert Chevara's production of Williams's *In the Bar of a Tokyo Hotel*, of which Chevara says: "The earlier plays are linear, whereas the later are largely experimental. I think that's why the critics at the time reacted with such bewilderment and incomprehension at Williams' new departure" (http://thisweeklondon.com/article/robert-chevara-in-the-bar-of-a-tokyo-hotel/).

If Kirk and Capitani are Williams's twenty-first-century saviors, Peter Hall held that title for the second half of the twentieth century, an earlier version of those Brits to champion Williams in Europe, or at least in the United Kingdom. Hall staged *Camino Real* at the Phoenix Theatre on April 8, 1957, and, almost immediately thereafter, an unexpurgated production of *Cat on a Hot Tin Roof*, but not without doing battle with the Lord Chamberlain again as he had done with Beckett's *Godot*. Hall's censored *Godot* would finally appear in the West End, and it accelerated profound, postwar European and American influences on the insular British stage that were already in place, led by Williams in 1948–49. Beckett would remain a central part of that cross-channel force, doing battle once again with the Lord Chamberlain over his next play, *Endgame*,[11] in 1957, as the Lord Chamberlain's office seemed determined to ensure that British theatre remain shy, genteel, un-modern, its ethos part of, if not mired within, an earlier era.

Similarly, Alessandro Clericuzio observed that

> When Luchino Visconti decided to direct Tennessee Williams' *The Glass Menagerie* in Rome in 1946, Italian theaters were slowly recovering—culturally and economically—from the ravages of World War II. Intellectuals were disappointed by the poorness of what Italian playwrights produced and disturbed by what audiences loved most (variety shows), while theatergoers were often offended by the lack of Italian plays in favor of foreign ones, and sometimes outraged by the themes these dramatic works offered to the public. (Clericuzio, 2014)

And yet, Italians had their own reservations: Of the early productions of *Un Tram che si chiama desiderio* (*A Streetcar Named Desire*), for instance, Clericuzio calls attention to "the prudery of Italians in the late 1940s" (Clericuzio, 77). His examples include the way the Italian press handled the homosexuality of Blanche's late husband, Allan Grey: "some were outraged, defining Allan's homosexuality as his 'beastly vice,' calling him 'depraved'" (Clericuzio, 77).

Using fresh archival material, Clericuzio goes on to examine the Italian reception to the famous film version of *Streetcar* (1951). Even as the promotional posters of the wildly popular film featured depictions of passion and images of Marlon Brando *en déshabillé*, the film itself was pre-sanitized by Hollywood. All reference to homosexuality and what many consider Kowalski's rape of his sister-in-law while his wife was in labor were expunged. The Italian dubbing of the film's dialogue had, furthermore, "'been transformed' […] 'where the literal translations are most injudicious'" (88), and the posters carried notices that tickets would not be sold to customers 16 years or younger. That was the (very) small print; the poster's imagery, on the other hand, proclaimed the film's principal appeal, selling sex. Clericuzio details the backstory of that age restriction with impressive research, digging into Italian archives and reviewing contemporary assessments. He concludes: "Six years after the birth of the Republic [in 1945], Italian entertainment was still controlled by two former Fascists who were profoundly linked to the Church and to [Giulio] Andreotti, 'who had in mind to crush Italian cinema.' […] Politics and the church, together with compliant bureaucrats, kept Italian culture (mainly popular culture) under very strict control" (87–88).

Such re-sanitizing of a film already pre-sanitized by Hollywood's Hays Code gives credence to Clericuzio's subtitle, "A Transcultural Perspective," although his perspective may more accurately be dubbed "bicultural" or "cross-cultural." Clericuzio's reception history might have been more transcultural, however, since the Italian reception of Williams was not unique, and resistance to his work was echoed in any number of other European countries as well, including the UK during the time when the Lord Chamberlain's reach extended to the approval of public performances. But Clericuzio details Williams's reception in Italy, particularly in the face of resistance from the Catholic Church and those who projected and protected its values:

> The late 1950s and early 1960s were years of quite harsh opposition to any artistic expression that seemed to deviate from the norm of Catholic and middle-class ethics. Italian censorship worked in many ways, not all of them explicit, towards […] "scandalous" artists as Pasolini […] et al.] Politicians, as well as some intellectuals, were trying to keep at bay forces of change that were about to explode from 1968 on. (184)

Clericuzio's detailed account of Williams's reception in Italy thus outlines many of the reasons why this very American, even regionally American, playwright had such wide, if often conflicted, appeal abroad. Despite the resistance of the Catholic Church, European artists, intellectuals, and general audiences may have accepted him more fully than American audiences, and his continued, if not continuous, performance in Europe suggests a richer vitality than the playwright seems to enjoy in his native land.

Despite some persistent resistance to Williams in the United Kingdom of the 1940s and 1950s, where his early publications were censored, his overall reception in Europe has been more consistently appreciative and receptive than it has been in his native United States. It has been especially so in the United Kingdom and Italy, but also across national borders and cultural boundaries into Sweden and France. In his native land he has too often been seen more as a curiosity than as the towering theatrical artist that he was. Of later plays like *The Two-Character Play*, Kirk notes, a bit moralizingly:

> It was just completely missed, the point of the play, because of American baggage and morality. Well we don't think like that. And that's what I've said about the plays we're doing here at Jermyn St and the plays they're doing at the Cock is that after a period of time we are suitably mature enough, and our minds changed enough, to go back to plays that have failed. Because plays do not always fail because they're rubbish, they fail because they are ahead of their time, and people cannot cope with them.

Ruby Cohn echoes such a call for reevaluation through performance. "What I think we have to do is to get productions for some of these later plays. […] I think one has to look at the versions and see good productions. *Clothes for a Summer Hotel*, for instance. I think it's a lovely play, but evidently the initial production was a nightmare. When will a director undertake to do it well?" (Bray, 2002, 27).

Chapter 4

REFRAMING TENNESSEE: A SHORT AFTERWORD

Felice: You will not, you must never look at an audience before a performance. It makes you play self-consciously, you don't get lost in the play. […]

Clare: Are you going to throw new speeches at me tonight?

Felice: Tonight there'll have to be a lot of improvisation, but if we're both lost in the play, the bits of improvisation won't matter at all, in fact they may make the play better.

—*The Two-Character Play* (10–11)

I see a multitude […] in transports […] of joy.

—*Endgame*

"Becoming Beckett" is a designation neither of disparagement nor of belatedness. It suggests, further, neither a creative decline nor a character deficiency. It is rather an expression of one of the creative multitudes that comprised Tennessee Williams, who was several. Its emphasis is on "becoming," to suggest, after Gilles Deleuze, an immanence, a continuous creative exploration and development, a process that Williams expected directors and actors to continue. Beckett is used here as an image of theatrical experiment and as a recognizable instance of such becoming. A revolutionary theatrical gesture like Beckett's *Waiting for Godot,* for instance, ought not freeze its author's talents, nor condemn an artist to a career of devising sequels, although sequels can themselves break new ground, as Beckett demonstrated with his follow-up theatrical enterprise, *Endgame.* Beckett considered this sequel to be, on one level, the story of Vladimir and Estragon at a later stage of their existence. Terence Killeen changes the terms of Beckett's equation, observing in the *Irish Times* during the 2020 pandemic lockdown that "*Endgame* is what would now be called a 'spin-off,'" and, further, "Hamm is a more reduced Pozzo: by the second act of *Godot*, Pozzo is already blind and barely able to

Figure 4.1 *Endgame* by Complicité (2009) with Simon McBurney as Clov (l) and Mark Rylance as Hamm (r)

walk; here in *Endgame* he is confined irrevocably to a chair."[1] One can quibble with Killeen's easy allegory and offer, instead, the position that *Endgame* broke sharply with *Godot*, as it turned theater back on itself. Beckett's theater followed his narrative art toward its famed self-reflexivity, but one might say as well that both readings (or viewings) pertain. Like Beckett's, much of Williams's later work is theater as theater, theater as subject of theater. Clare: "You're terrible with the press, you go on and on about *total theatre*" (*The Two-Character Play*, 5). Moreover, both authors have altered theater imagery decidedly. When Mark Rylance and Simon McBurney staged *Endgame* in 2009 with Complicité,[2] it looked to have come directly from the sweaty T-shirt imagery of Tennessee Williams, either from *A Streetcar Named Desire* or even from *The Two-Character Play*.[3] The setting for *Godot*, furthermore, is "a country road. A tree. Evening"; that for *The Two-Character Play*, "an evening in an unspecified locality."

Whether or not Beckett's later plays, some miniatures, most "undramatic," others "unreadable," signal a creative falling off, or, on the contrary, the aggressive advance of a project to refashion theatre remains a point of contention among some critics and audiences, and much of that hesitancy or uncertainty is punctuated by commercial timidity, a reluctance to stage some of the later experimental, exploratory shorts. The commercial theater for Beckett, as it does for Williams, remains dominated by the major early works, even as gems are to be found among the later work of both playwrights. Two experimental Williams plays opened at the Longacre Theatre on Broadway in February 1966 under the very Beckettian title, *Slapstick Tragedy*, directed by Beckett's primary American director, Alan Schneider. What might have been a creative breakthrough, however, ran for only seven performances. Schneider would direct both phases of Edward Albee's career, as well: the drawing room excoriations of academic couples, *Who's Afraid of Virginia Woolf?*, in 1962, and the most experimental of Albee's work, *Box* and *Quotations from Chairman Mao Tse-Tung*, at the Billie Rose Theatre on Broadway in November 1968. The latter was part of a repertory project called *Theater 1969* that included Albee's "absurdist" *Sandbox* and Beckett's *Krapp's Last Tape*, among other short Albee works. *Box*, too, may overlap with Beckett, Albee's "Becoming Beckett," in that it is a play without characters, not unlike Beckett's 30-second playlet *Breath*. Williams described what he thought of as a theatrical diversion in a preface to *Slapstick Tragedy* published by *Esquire*:[4]

> I believe that the peculiar style of these two short plays is accurately defined by their mutual title. They are not "Theatre of The Absurd"; they are short, fantastic works whose content is a dislocated and wildly idiomatic sort of tragedy, perhaps a bit like the feature stories in that newspaper, the *National Enquirer*, which I think is the finest journalistic review of the precise time that we live in. The style of the plays is kin to vaudeville, burlesque and slapstick, with a dash of pop art thrown in. (95)

Something of the same might be said of *Waiting for Godot*, save the *National Enquirer* comment, which comment may reflect Williams's persistent interest in the Gothic, Southern or other. *Esquire* also published both plays in the issue, *The Mutilated* (96) [by a mastectomy] and *The Gnädiges Fräulein* (102) [figurative German for "The Blessed Virgin"], said Fräulein offering "the best stage soliloquy since Hamlet."

For Williams, the majority of professional theater critics have disparaged such experimental later work to the point of cruelty. "White Dwarf's Tragic Fade Out" is an excoriating review of *In the Bar of a Tokyo Hotel* published in the June 1969 issue of *Life* magazine.[5] Reviewer and *Time* associate editor Stefan Kanfer details what he calls Williams's extinction using the astronomical image of a white dwarf star: "Tennessee Williams appears to be a White Dwarf," a star dead but still sending light to the earth. Those messages, however, "come from a cinder"; "nothing about the work justifies its production, least of all its plot"; the play's protagonist, like its author, "a once gifted man"; "Williams believes that with this sophistic exercise he is laying his life on the line, delineating the role of the creator in an indifferent or hostile world." The only consolation offered is that "it is possible that the author is in temporary decline," although, finally, Kanfer notes that "Williams is caught looking in his rear-view mirror" (11–12). And the magazine went further, taking out a full-page ad in the *New York Times* featuring a photograph of Williams beneath which the caption read, "Played Out" (Saddik, 2015, 15).[6] Writing in *Variety* in November of 1996, Greg Evans goes after the revival of Williams's failed and much-rewritten 1970s work *The Red Devil Battery Sign*. Evans's piece is little more than a mugging with requisite *ad hominem* assault: "The much-abused reputation of Tennessee Williams' late plays won't be redeemed by the WPA Theater's revival of 'The Red Devil Battery Sign.' A tale of paranoia and intrigue in the aftermath of the JFK assassination, the 1973 'Devil' is itself a paranoid *mélange* of apocalyptic nightmare and fluttery panic, as if Blanche DuBois had been plunked into the latest Oliver Stone film. With its shock value all but evaporated (conspiracy theories aren't what they used to be), 'Devil' is left with a depressing barrage of unintended self-parody" (Evans, 1996).

Ben Brantley described *The Two-Character Play* as "Tennessee Williams's rarely seen fever dream of an eternal *folie à deux*," and continues:

> The reality-and-illusion games à la Pirandello that are played here were old hat even when Williams began working on *The Two-Character Play* in the 1960s. I certainly can't defend it as a cohesive or entirely original work of art. By the end of its much weaker second act, when its symbols overpower its people, it has come to feel like a goulash of avant-garde leftovers. (Brantley, 2013)

Such responses to Williams's late plays, what legendary Beckett scholar Ruby Cohn calls Williams's inability "to evoke a kind word from critics" (234), too often constituted little more than attacks on his character, personality, lifestyle,[7] or, like Brantley, on misconceptions about his theater explorations. Of these, some were exercises in dialogue or movement (see Beckett's ballet *Quad* in this regard), some featuring direct addresses to the audience (see Beckett's "A Piece of Monologue" in this regard), others spotlit monologues not unlike Beckett's *Play*, or even Wallace Shawn's *The Designated Mourner*. On the other hand, when Cohn tells a panel of dedicated Williams scholars that "I think *Out Cry* [i.e., *The Two-Character Play*] is […] influenced by Beckett" (Bray, 2002, 29), she is issuing praise, high praise at that. Williams, in fact, considered *The Two-Character Play* to be his "most beautiful play since *Streetcar* and I've never stopped working on it […] It is a *cri de coeur*, but then all creative work, all life, in a sense is a *cri de coeur*."[8] Citing Gunn on the *Out Cry/ The Two-Character Play* revisions, Cohn accents Williams's proclivity to rewrite continuously: "Three versions of this play were published [1969, 1973, and 1976 in vol. v] (and more produced). In general those titled *The Two-Character Play* are among the most interesting of Williams's final period; that entitled *Out Cry* is among the worst" (238). Cohn notes further that the Gunn "bibliography mentions over sixty titles of unpublished Williams plays in manuscript collections" (232), at least as of 1991,[9] and offers something of a path to redemption, as she notes that "directors and actors continue to discover what critics have cast aside as self-repetition" (232).

If the primary thread of this volume is a rethinking or reframing of Williams's work as experimental from the first, one image of which is T-shirt Modernism (see Chapter 1), the other thread is that producers and directors outside the United States have been more willing to explore his works, early and late, without the predispositions that tend to accompany his reputation in the United States (see Chapters 2 and 3). To see Williams as imitative of his predecessors, moreover, constitutes a reductive misreading, as the early works owe a certain but not imitative debt to Elmer Rice, Clifford Odets, and even Eugene O'Neill, as William Inge owes a certain but not imitative debt to Williams (see Chapter 1). One might say something of the same for Arthur Miller.[10] Williams's later, more overtly experimental theater exercises may suggest certain affinities with European experimentalists, but that suggests creative movement into areas opened by other artists rather than repetition or imitation. That opening of theatrical possibilities is the acknowledged debt of Inge and Miller to Williams. The final tributes are performances, however, which one hopes will be spurred by certain scholarly reexaminations, especially in a book series designated as "Impact Books."

Case Studies

Saddik reviews one such American rethinking of Williams for the *Tennessee Williams Annual Review*, the 2017 Mabou Mines (with Piece by Piece) adaptation called *Glass Guignol: The Brother and Sister Play*. The production "frames its central action through the brother-sister duo in *The Two-Character Play*"[11] among its interlacing of material from Williams and others, including Sigmund Freud, Mary Shelley, and E. T. A. Hoffmann. Saddik cites the group's website, where they explain something of their theatrical philosophy, which the site calls director Lee "Breuer's always surprising take on classic texts":[12] "iconic passages of Williams' dialogue reframed in an unfamiliar context tell a hidden story of his sister Rose. Fear, creativity—and monsters within and without" (paragraph 4). Unsurprisingly, perhaps, some of the imagery echoes Beckett's *Endgame* and other Beckett adaptations that Mabou Mines has staged over its 50-year creative tenure of reframing theater.

Among the few productions that thoroughly rethought and so reframed Williams during the centenary year was Breuer's Paris staging of *A Streetcar Named Desire*. Of the worldwide attention paid to Williams in 2011, one of the most notable examples was that from the land of Molière. France celebrated the centenary with a new production of Williams's most famous and oft-produced play in a new French translation by Jean-Michel Déprats, which superseded

Figure 4.2 Lee Breuer's *Un tramway nommé Désir* [*A Streetcar Named Desire*] at the Comedie-Française, 2014

the 1949 adaptation by Jean Cocteau and Paule de Beaumont, *Un tramway nommé Désir*. Breuer's 2011 French production was the first American play to be staged at the house of Molière, the staid Comédie-Française, in its 330-year history. It was offered there from February 5 to June 2, 2011. Much of the credit for so bold a move, particularly so given the radical nature of the production, is due to the theater's innovative artistic director, Muriel Mayette, herself a fan of the American director. In Breuer's hands, *Un tramway nommé Désir* is relocated from a seedy, postwar New Orleans to sixteenth-century Japan, featuring *dogugaeshi*-inspired sliding screens and *kuroko* stagehands reminiscent of *bunraku* puppeteers. Breuer notes that these are "a metaphor for the antebellum South" (11), adding another level of chronological pastiche to the time where the kimono-clad Blanche's sensibility lay, or rather where it remains stuck.[13] On his web page, designer Basil Twist and collaborator Breuer emphasize the cinematic features of the 2011 staging: "Painted screens of varying sizes were displayed in rapid succession. Many were magnificent paintings in themselves. This was a cinematographic art form of incomparable beauty. In Twist's award-winning original work, 'Dogugaeshi,' he utilized the Awajashima screens in a modern context. [...] the Dogugaeshi screens become the cinematic homage to *Streetcar Named Desire*." Breuer's theatrical conception seems much less *outré* once we consider Williams's description of Stella's putting on "a light[14] blue satin kimono" and Blanche's having similarly "slipped into a dark red satin wrapper" [kimono?] (50, 53).

For his celebratory, international centenary production, Breuer was doubtless aware of the French premiere, the controversial 1949 Jean Cocteau adaptation. Williams was finally offended by Cocteau's radical departures and racialized adaptation in Raymond Rouleau's staging:

> I don't understand why Cocteau filled my work with crudities. I don't think it's enough to put a refrigerator on the stage or to make the actors speak like the common public [that is, in a French street argot] so as to give a more vivid impression. Art is not a photograph. Truth and life cannot be expressed in their essence except when we transmute them. (*Les Nouvelles littéraires*, June 8, 1950, cited in Dubois, 134)

For example, Cocteau would feature Black dancers, naked from the waist up, gyrating in the background as Stanley raped Blanche (Kolin, 2000, 70–76). His introduction to the play came close to justifying its sexual violence, or at least he placed the emphasis squarely on Blanche as seductress. "The press spoke much about rapes. Strange. Where did it see them? In a husband who reconciles himself with his wife? In Stanley, who takes advantage of Blanche's weakness in a scene when she *resists him only for form's sake*?" (emphasis added; see appendix in Kontaxopoulos [2001]). Cocteau, moreover, added a second, mimed rape in the background, suggesting, what, how common a feature sexual aggression is in this uncivilized part of the world, where animals rule? Williams would certainly have found Breuer's stylized production decidedly less vulgar than Cocteau's, and Breuer and Twist worked to evoke New Orleans for his French audience with an image of an olive green, New Orleans streetcar hanging above a jazz band, but whether Williams would have recognized the play as his own amid Breuer's adaptations remains an open question. When the doctors come for her, Blanche (played in 2011 by Anne Kessler to Éric Ruf's Stanley) falls through a trap door, presumably to her death, and the sisters' physical affection for each other borders on the incestuous.

Streetcar has, admittedly, had more daring, transformative adaptations and reframings than Breuer's—or Cocteau's, for that matter. A case in point is Krzysztof Warlikowski's production of *Un Tramway, creation d'après Un Tramway nommé Désir de Tennessee Williams*, with the incomparable and well-dressed Isabelle Huppert. This was produced at the Novwy Teatr—Varsowie and ran at the Théâtre Odéon from February 4 to April 3, 2010, featuring scenes in a contemporary bowling alley, video projections, and explicit, presumably simulated, onstage sex. Like Cocteau, Warlikowski liberally adapted a new text, in this case by Lebanese-Canadian (Québécois) author and director Wajdi Mouawad. Similarly, Frank Castorf's notorious 2002 Berlin Volksbühne version was entitled not *Endstation Sehnsucht*, with the sense of a "terminal" or a final stop

Figure 4.3 Lee Breuer's *Un tramway nommé Désir* [*A Streetcar Named Desire*] at the Comedie-Française, 2014

already built into the original German translation, but *Endstation Amerika* [*A Streetcar Named America*, but also "End of the line America," or America as the end of the line]. This was a shortened form of *Endstation Amerika: Eine Bearbeitung von Frank Castorf von Endstation Sehnsucht—A Streetcar Named Desire von Tennessee Williams*. This awkward title resulted from the executors of the Williams estate disallowing the use of Williams's title for Castorf's radical departures from the text. In his blog, Ivar Hagendoorn characterizes some of the alterations thus:

> In Castorf's adaptation Stanley Kowalski is a Polish immigrant who used to stand on the barricades alongside Lech Walesa. Those were the days. He now earns a living handing people chewing gum samples on the street. He makes some extra money with the illegal export of liquor. In one scene Blanche compares him to a gorilla. A moment later Stanley enters in a gorilla costume. It is his working outfit. This scene perfectly illustrates Stanley Kowalski's personal tragedy and the subtle layers Frank Castorf has added to the piece.

Whether Castorf's addition of Stanley in a gorilla suit is subtle by anyone's measure or whether it "perfectly illustrates Stanley Kowalski's personal tragedy" is at least a debatable point. At very least something of Stanley's American patriotism and his status as an American World War II veteran get lost in making him Polish rather than Polish-American. It remains a measure of the play's power that critics saw such updating and Europianization in positive terms, an enrichment of the play rather than a diminishment. Even so, much of what Brooks Atkinson calls a "genuinely poetic playwright" may get lost in the adaptation of the play to an East German setting. That setting is itself ironic in that the German translation was done in West Germany, as a political example of liberal, uncensored, free expression as much as for the play's own aesthetic qualities. But such radical adaptations (if not a travesty in Castorf's case) may be inevitable in German productions, since Berthold Viertel's original German translation *Endstation Sehnsucht*, still readily available, contains so many errors, having been done quickly in postwar West Germany (Clericuzio, 2016, 80–81).

As international and transgressive as Breuer's 2011 French production was, that by the Sydney Theater Company was traditional and displayed a play less in need of adaptation or renovation than one that continues to attract the highest level of actors and devoted audiences.[15] It opened its production of *Streetcar* in Liv Ullmann's 2009 "blazing revival" (*Vogue Daily*, November 2009) at the Kennedy Center in Washington, DC, in November before moving in December to the Harvey Theater of the Brooklyn Academy of Music in New York with Cate Blanchett as Blanche DuBois. Its short New York run, between November 27 and December 20, sold out instantly as soon as the notice appeared online. Writing for the *New York Times*, Ben Brantley gushed:

> Ms. Ullmann and Ms. Blanchett have performed the play as if it had never been staged before, with the result that, as a friend of mine put it, "you feel like you're hearing words you thought you knew pronounced correctly for the first time." [...] how often do you get to watch an actress of such virtuosity pulling out every stop of her instrument and then some?

For Brantley, such a production was "Blessed perhaps with an outsider's distance on an American cultural monument."

In the wake of the 2011 Williams centenary, Italian director Antonio Latella reframed *Un tram che si chiama Desiderio* through the lens of *The Glass Menagerie* (*Lo zoo di vetro*), with Laura Marinoni as Blanche and Vinicio Marchioni as Stanley, which opened in Modena in February of 2012. Latella also used the fresh Masolino D'Amico retranslation of the play that was premiered at the Festival dei Due Mondi's Teatro San Nicolò di Spoleto on July 2, 1993, but with a twist. *Un tram che si chiama Desiderio* became a memory play for Latella, Blanche's recollections, her retrospective after her commitment to the mental institution that ends Williams's conception of the play. That shift was signaled visually from the first with a set that combined the hospital setting where Blanche

Figure 4.4 Vinicio Marchioni as Stanley channeling Brando in Antonio Latella's 2011, *Un tram che si chiama Desiderio* [*A Streetcar Named Desire*]. Photo by Brunella Giolivo

has been living since the end of *Streetcar*, a film set for the 1951 film complete with visible sound crew and cameramen, and the Kowalski apartment in New Orleans with period appointments. In Blanche's reenactment of events, she is a willing participant in what is generally considered, by Williams in particular, the play's culminating rape. Here she assumes the superior position in this extended, explicit sexual simulation where Blanche is the more active partner. Moreover, the closing image of this production is an eroticized Blanche sitting in the lap of the hospital doctor, the encounter suggesting an ongoing sexual relationship.

In May of 2013, when the touring production of the play opened at the Piccolo Teatro in Milan, I was invited to deliver a preproduction lecture and to participate in a postproduction talkback with the cast. The invitation came on the basis, presumably, of my recently released bilingual edition of the play from Edizioni ETS in Pisa in 2012, the release just missing the Williams centenary as well. I had wanted to use the D'Amico translation of the play for that volume, but Giulio Einaudi Editore, Williams's Italian publisher, insisted I use the traditional Gerardo Guerrieri translation. The preproduction talk went well enough, something of a standard overview of the play's production history and principal themes, but I had not seen the production beforehand. When during the postproduction talkback I outlined what I considered deviations from the Williams script, the cast leapt to the defense of the play and its director, insisting that not a word of Williams's script had been changed. The discussion highlighted the fundamental paradox of theater, its mix of communication systems. In theater, the text, the playwright's script, is not the dominant system. In Latella's staging, the script had essentially been superseded by the powerful visuals in terms of set, with

Figure 4.5 Laura Marinoni as a sexually superior Blanche in Antonio Latella's 2011 *Un tram che si chiama Desiderio* [*A Streetcar Named Desire*]. Photo by Brunella Giolivo

massive, punishing Klieg lights and mimed, unscripted actions. But Latella seems to have taken his cue from lines like Blanche's "I called him a little boy and laughed and flirted. Yes, I was flirting with your husband," while all but ignoring lines like "The first time I laid eyes on him I thought to myself, that man is my executioner. That man will destroy me...," which sounds less prescient and ominous amid this retrospective, psychologically-layered setting. Latella had effectively reframed or refashioned Williams, both echoing the history of Williams's theater by invoking *The Glass Menagerie* and further emphasizing Williams's immense impact through film. All of this amounted to substantial recasting and rewriting of the stage plays for their film versions, none more extreme than the film version of *A Streetcar Named Desire* that the *Guardian*'s Ed Pilkington calls "the black-and-white splendour of the 1951 film version" and the happy ending grafted onto Richard Brooks's 1962 film version of *Sweet Bird of Youth*. In an echo of *Streetcar*'s acting tradition, moreover, Marchioni's Stanley wore the requisite T-shirt, but, channeling Marlon Brando, perhaps, one imprinted with Brando's image. It was a *tour de force*.

The intertextual pastiche and theatrical reframing that Breuer and Latella effected reflect Ruby Cohn's insistent call for more attention to the later plays, first in her 1997 essay on the late plays for the *Cambridge Companion*, then repeated at a roundtable discussion at the New Orleans Tennessee Williams

Festival in 2002: "What I think we have to do is to get productions for some of these later plays. [...] I think one has to look at the versions and see good productions" (Bray, 27). In his preface to *Slapstick Tragedy*, Williams details the importance of the theatrical process to his creative production, in this case of "Ten Blocks on the Camino Real":

> A short sketch of that play was published in a paperback called *American Blues*[16] and Elia Kazan happened to come across it and thought it would be fun to do as an Actors Studio exercise. As he and the actors played around with it, Kazan found himself becoming excited by its offbeat style, and when I came through New York, on my way to Rome, he suggested that I drop by the studio to see what Eli Wallach and two or three other highly gifted players had made of the sketch. 1 was truly amazed. Kazan had found precisely the right key of the little sketch and had invested it with his brilliantly inventive exuberance. Right then and there we decided to put it on Broadway, and I began to expand it into a full-length play.

If we expect Williams to continue recasting the postwar masculinity we have dubbed T-shirt Modernism, we are bound to be disappointed with Williams's continued becoming, his "Becoming Beckett," his other Williamses. As Cohn suggests, we need someone to continue to "play around" with these pieces and to find "precisely the right key" for them.

NOTES

Saint Tennessee: An Introduction

1 Contextually it is worth noting that the Battle of the Bulge, the Ardennes offensive in Belgium, America's largest and bloodiest battle of World War II, was still in doubt.

2 Rose would die of a heart attack in September of 1996 at the Phelps Memorial Hospital in Tarrytown, New York, at the age of 86. She thus outlived her younger brother and financial supporter by some 13 years. See critic Mel Gussow's obituary in the "Arts" section of the *New York Times*, September 7, 1996.

3 See Isaacs, "Burlesque, According to Reinhardt," p. 697, and "Burlesque Stuff: A series of four drawings by Kenneth Hartwell," pp. 749–52, especially p. 752.

4 As Brick says, "Maybe that's why you put Maggie and me in this room that was Jack Straw's and Peter Ochello's, in which that pair of old sisters slept in a double bed where both of 'em died!" (86).

5 Savran cited on the Saddik book jacket.

Chapter 1 T-Shirt Modernism and Performed Masculinities: The Theatrical Refashionings of Tennessee Williams and William Inge

1 For a seriocomic glimpse of this life, see the Williams's poem "Life Story," which ends, like a Williams play, "Auto-da-Fé," perhaps, with the line, "and that's how people burn to death in hotel rooms." *The Collected Poems of Tennessee Williams*. New York: New Directions, 2002.

2 Selected for inclusion in *The Best One-Act Plays of 1941*, ed. Margaret Mayorga, 1942. This would be Williams's second selection in this annual series, "Moony's Kid Don't Cry" having appeared in *The Best One-Act Plays of 1940*. Under the title, "Three Plays by Tennessee Williams: Moony's Kid Don't Cry/The Last of My Solid Gold Watches/ This Property Is Condemned," the evening of short plays was directed by Sidney Lumet for the live TV series, "Kraft Theatre," on April 16, 1958.

3 Further, see the ending to "Portrait of a Madonna," who exhibits Blanche-like fantasies and finally shares Blanche's fate.

4 See also Lahr (2014, 102) for further details and a photo. Lahr uses the term "primitive" to describe the tempestuous Pancho.

5 See also Enelow (2019) on sweat.

6   Tellingly, the first Signet edition (with the Thomas Hart Benton cover) includes a photo of the French production (facing 73), the French adaptation directed by Jean Cocteau. Yves Vincent as Stanley (with Arletty as Blanche), however, seems without the charisma generated by the T-shirt-wearing Brando. This photo is dropped from the next Signet edition that features not the Benton painting but a buff Brando on the cover.

7   The 1962 Penguin edition of the three plays (and its 1985 reprint) uses a photo of Vivien Leigh and Bonar Colleano from the 1949 Aldwych Theatre production, directed by Leigh's then-husband, Laurence Olivier.

8   See "National Theatre Is Authorized by Congress to Advance the Drama; Distinguished Patrons of the Stage Are Named as Incorporators—Art of the Theatre to Be Developed by School and Productions throughout the Country." https://www.nytimes.com/1935/06/30/archives/national-theatre-is-authorized-by-congress-to-advance-the-drama.html?sq=%2522American%2520National%2520Theatre%2520and%2520Academy%2522&scp=2&st=cse.

9   Like Williams, Odets was capable of certain commercialism as well as he moved from political commitment to write the screenplay for the 1961 film, *Wild in the Country*, an adaptation of J. R. Salamanca's 1958 novel, *The Lost Country*. The film starred Elvis Pressley and Hope Land, and featured, of course, songs by Pressley. In "Random Observations," a preface to the 1941 play, *Stairs to the Roof*, Williams already had his eye on Hollywood, noting that the play was "written for both the stage and the screen" with hopes of Burgess Meredith as the lead.

10 *Stairs to the Roof* would first be performed in 1945 in a laboratory setting to an invited audience of the Pasadena Playbox, a venue accommodating some fifty audience members, the play moving to a full production at the larger Pasadena Playhouse on February 26, 1947. *Streetcar* would open on Broadway some ten months later.

11 Rice himself finally directed the very successful Broadway production.

12 See Isaacs, "Settings for Machinal: Two Designs," p. 704.

13 Called "dumbbell Ruth" in the tabloids, Ruth Snyder was executed in the electric chair at New York's Sing Sing Prison on January 12, 1928. http://www.nydailynews.com/news/crime/ruthless-ruth-article-1.344029.

14 See play text in *Theatre Arts Monthly*, vol. 12, no. 10 (October 1928), p. 704. The Grand Theatre of Blackpool, UK, has named *Machinal* one of the ten "Best Theatre Plays of All Time," "which are still important for today's audiences." Machinal, then, is here in the company of *Oedipus Rex*, Marlowe's *Faustus*, *Hamlet*, and *A Streetcar Named Desire*. The Blackpool web page also includes a trailer for the 2008 Royal National Theatre of London's revival of *Machinal*: https://www.blackpoolgrand.co.uk/best-theatre-plays-time/. Accessed April 9, 2021.

15 Manuscript and typescript numbers are those used in Loomis to correspond to the system at the Humanities Research Center at the University of Texas, Austin.

16 Published together, "Two complete full length novels" by Signet in 1954 (S1109).

17 Williams's memory may have failed him some here. Lahr has the play that Inge read and Williams recommended to his agent, Audrey Wood, as Inge's first play, *Farther off from Heaven* (Lahr, 2014, 406), the play produced by Margo Jones for "Theater '47" in Dallas, Texas, in 1947. *Come Back, Little Sheba* came to Broadway in 1950. A decade after its Dallas premiere, Inge would rework *Farther off from Heaven* into *The Dark at the Top of the Stairs* (1957), directed by Elia Kazan, for the publication of which Williams would write an introduction (q.v.).

18   See the playscript and a film photo montage in *Theatre Arts*, vol. 40, no. 10 (October 1956), pp. 33–59.

19   See also Maruéjouls-Koch (2017).

20   As an apprentice film writer in Hollywood, Faulkner's treatments and scripts remained mostly unproduced, and he received early screen credit for only two films, both written in 1944: *To Have and Have Not* (produced 1945) and *The Big Sleep* (produced 1946)— both starring Humphrey Bogart and Lauren Bacall. Scholars have had access to the former, but Herbert Mitgang reports that no copies of the latter have been found (see Herbert Mitgang, "A Trove of Faulkner Film Scripts." *New York Times*, July 28, 1987, 11. https://www.nytimes.com/1987/07/28/movies/a-trove-of-faulkner-film-scripts.html). But see Garrett, George P., Jr., O. B. Hardison and Jane R. Gelfman (eds.), *Film Scripts One: Henry V, The Big Sleep, A Streetcar Named Desire—Classic Screenplays*. New York: Applause Theatre and Cinema Books, 2013. After the award of the Nobel Prize in 1949, film interest in Faulkner's own stories increased. For *The Long Hot Summer* (1958) Faulkner is cited both for story and screenwriting. *The Sound and the Fury* followed in 1959, but Faulkner is not credited as a screen writer. In terms of imagery, the 1944 films reflect a "tie and jacket" world; the 1958 film is T-shirt Modernism.

21   The role went, of course, to James Dean, but Brando's screen test is now available at: https://www.youtube.com/watch?v=p8x90gYM1Vs. The issue of who was imitating whose acting style is entertained at: https://faroutmagazine.co.uk/rare-footage-of-marlon-brandos-original-screen-test-for-rebel-without-a-cause/.

22   See, for example, https://en.wikipedia.org/wiki/Category:American_plays_adapted_into_films.

23   See https://www.pulitzer.org/article/memoriam-sam-shepard-1943-2017.

24   For Williams's contemplation of such theatrical hybridity and a move toward a more "plastic" theater in the period immediately after *A Streetcar Named Desire*, see Maruéjouls-Koch (2014).

25   See, for example, http://bookscans.com/Publishers/signet/signet.htm and https://surface.syr.edu/cgi/viewcontent.cgi?article=1193&context=libassoc. "'Portrait of a Madonna' (1944) depicts an aging, self-deluding belle with elements of both Blanche Dubois and Alma Winemiller of 'Summer and Smoke.' It was in an early production of 'Portrait of a Madonna,' in fact, that Jessica Tandy, later to portray Blanche so memorably, first entered the world of Williams." Samuel G. Freedman, "A Playwright's Early Works Offer Glimpses of His Later Genius." *New York Times*, May 18, 1986. https://www.nytimes.com/1986/05/18/theater/a-playwright-s-early-works-offer-glimpses-of-his-later-genius.html. For a photograph of Tandy in this role, see Grissom (2015, 107).

Chapter 2 "Intense Honesty": Race, Sex and Cross-Cultural Perspectives

1   Details in my *Un tram che si chiama desiderio/ A Streetcar Named Desire. Canone teatrale europeo/ Canon of European Drama*. Volume No. 7 in the book series.

2   For the New York productions, see https://www.ibdb.com/broadway-show/cat-on-a-hot-tin-roof-2442.

3   See discussion at https://blogs.bl.uk/americas/2020/02/from-the-collections-a-streetcar-named-desire.html.

4 The book version appeared from Oakville, Ontario (CA): Mosaic Press in 2002.

5 See Lahr's theatrical wish list for Christmas, December 22, 2011: https://www.newyorker.com/culture/culture-desk/the-best-theatre-of-the-year.

See also the "prequel" to Lahr's position where he objects to other forms of textual alterations: "To replace the Jewish Willy Loman with an African-American is to change something elemental in the nature of the play's lament": https://www.newyorker.com/magazine/2009/05/25/hard-sell.

See further Lahr's 2012 objections to further tampering with Williams's work, *In Masks Outrageous and Austere* (directed by David Schweizer, at the Culture Project).

The show is billed as the "world première of Tennessee Williams' final full-length play." It is not *his* play; it is yet another regrettable co-authorship—a compilation of six different versions by six well-meaning collaborators and a computer [collation] program, Juxta [Commons], which conducted a "forensic analysis" of the text. To borrow a line from the script, "My God, if this were theatre, I'd think it a metaphor for the idiocy of existence." https://www.newyorker.com/magazine/2012/04/30/past-imperfect.

We should add that Lahr's *Tennessee Williams: Mad Pilgrimage of the Flesh* won the 2014 National Book Critics Circle Award for biography.

6 For details, see Kimberle Crenshaw, Neil Gotanda, Gary Peller and Kendall Thomas (eds.), *Critical Race Theory: The Key Writings That Formed the Movement* (New York: New Press, 1999).

7 A major exception is found in the notorious short story of cannibalism and homosexuality in "Desire and the Black Masseur," written in 1946 and so essentially concurrent with *A Streetcar Named Desire*. See also *Noir et Blanc*, the 1986 black-and-white film version adapted and directed by Claire Devers.

8 Nashville Ballet, however, hosted an American performance of Annabelle Lopez Ochoa's "narrative ballet," produced by the Scottish Ballet, of *Streetcar* in November 2019: https://www.pointemagazine.com/streetcar-named-desire-annabelle-lopez-ochoa-2641165926.html?rebelltitem=1#rebelltitem1.

The ballet had also been performed at the Spoleto Festival USA near Charleston, South Carolina in May of 2015: https://theartmag.com/2015/05/review-a-streetcar-named-desire/.

See also André Previn's 1998 opera version of *Streetcar*: https://www.operaamerica.org/applications/nawd/newworks/details.aspx?id=73.

Scheduled for performance by the Arizona Opera in February and March 2021. https://azopera.org/performances/streetcar-named-desire.

9 https://wtfestival.org/main-events/a-streetcar-named-desire/ and https://www.broadwayworld.com/article/Williamstown-Theatre-Festival-Announces-2020-Season-20200211.

10 For issues of the subsequent color line, see the politically charged musical (or opera) of 1950 by Langston Hughes, *The Barrier: A Musical Drama* adapted from his earlier Broadway success, *Mulatto*, the story of a southern white plantation owner living conjugally with his Black housekeeper. That relationship produced several light-skinned children who, nonetheless, must legally be classified as Mulatto and so face the racial divide, the barrier, what in 1926 Hughes called "the Racial Mountain," even within the family. It ran, also at the Broadhurst Theatre, from November 2–4, 1950. See also Hughes's poem "Cross": "I wonder where I'm gonna die/ Being neither

white nor black." See William Allen, "'The Barrier': A Critique," *Phylon (1940-1956)*, vol. 11, no. 2 (1950), pp. 134–36.

11 The play opened at Comedy Theatre on January 30, 1958, with Kim Stanley as Maggie, Paul Massie as Brick and Leo McKern as Big Daddy.

12 This club was founded in 1957 within the Comedy Theatre in order to stage an unexpurgated production of Arthur Miller's *A View from the Bridge* banned by the LC for its homosexual references. The following year, Hall's *Cat on a Hot Tin Roof* was produced there despite the LC's ban. See "'Cat on a Hot Tin Roof' beats the Censor, 1957–58." http://www.overthefootlights.co.uk/1957-58.pdf. That uncredited story also cites a Dublin theater manager's arrest for producing Williams's *The Rose Tattoo*, even as Dublin had no official theater censorship at the time.

13 For more on Sweden's role in early European performances of Williams's work, see publisher Lars Schmidt's dedicated website: https://www.loc.gov/collections/lars-schmidt/articles-and-essays/tennessee-williams/.

14 In 2005, Hall recalled that

> *Look Back in Anger* was a play formed by the careful naturalism of the 30s and the craft beloved by the old repertory theatres. It now looks dated and prolix because it uses the convention of the old well-made play. I think that my generation heard more political revolution in it than was actually there— largely because we desperately needed to.

See also the British Library's web page for a slightly different take on the play: https://www.bl.uk/works/look-back-in-anger.

15 See Leigh's contract for *A Streetcar Named Desire* at "Papers relating to H. M. Tennent," RP95, 2363, Theatre Museum, London.

16 See the American *Playbill* reproduced at: https://blogs.bl.uk/americas/2020/02/from-the-collections-a-streetcar-named-desire.html.

17 Letter on deposit at the Harry Ransom Humanities Research Center, University of Texas, Austin, Tennessee Williams Collection, box 59.7; see also the papers of his agent, Audrey Wood, in box 4.5.

18 Peter Hall's production of *Cat on a Hot Tin Roof* at the Watergate Theatre Club in January 1958 had and retained two intervals.

19 For images, see https://screenplaystv.wordpress.com/2015/01/12/cat-on-a-hot-tin-roof-1976/.

20 *Becoming Tennessee Williams*, 2011: https://www.hrc.utexas.edu/exhibitions/2011/becoming-tennessee-williams/.

21 See also British Library, Add MS 68871. Referenced Ts. p. 45 available for viewing at: https://blogs.bl.uk/untoldlives/2019/06/homosexuality-censorship-and-the-british-stage.html.

22 The British Museum's Olivier Archive also contains correspondence between Philip C. Kolin and the secretaries to Lord and Lady Olivier relating to a letter from Olivier to Tennessee Williams about the 1949 production of *Streetcar*, and including a copy of the letter, of which the original is now in the library of the University of Texas, 1989–90.

The University of Texas, Austin, also holds a mimeographed copy of the *Streetcar* script from 1949 in box 44.4 as well as a copy of Vivien Leigh's 1949 playscript from the Olivier production.

23   Ibid.; cited also in Philip C. Kolin, *Tennessee Williams: A Streetcar Named Desire* (Plays in Production series) (Cambridge: Cambridge University Press, 2000), p. 151. Documents held by the British Library and quotations cited via Creative Commons Non-Commercial License and the British Open Government License.

24   Irene Selznick, wife of movie mogul, David O. Selznick, covered some 25 percent of the show's $100,000 production costs. In 1947, as a birthday gift, David commissioned a painting of one of the play's scenes from American regionalist painter, Thomas Hart Benton, who painted the famous *Poker Night* scene now part of the Whitney Museum's permanent collection. https://whitney.org/collection/works/4174. The painting was subsequently used as the cover for the Signet paperback edition, and a detail was used for a Penguin reissue of the play in 2000, even as that published script for *A Streetcar Named Desire and Other Plays* was the one censored to conform with the Lord Chamberlain's objections, the full script unstaged in Britain until the mid-1980s.

25   British Library, Olivier Archive. Vol. CCLXIX (ff.). *A Streetcar Named Desire* by Tennessee Williams; produced by Olivier for Tennant Productions, starring Vivien Leigh as Blanche Dubois. First performance at the Aldwych, October 11, 1949.1. ff. Add MS 80034.

26   Maria Britneva (Maria St. Juste) would be his confidant for 35 years, his "Five-O'Clock Angel," and on whom he based the character of Maggie the Cat.

27   Also cited by Tennessee Williams in *Notebooks* (2007, 709).

28   See the *New York Times* article, March 17, 1957, called "Tennessee Williams on the Past, the Present and the Perhaps," reprinted as "The Past, Present and Perhaps" and used as an "Introduction" to the Signet edition of *The Fugitive Kind*, pp. v–ix.

29   Peter Brook would stage the Paris premiere of *Cat on a Hot Tin Roof* in 1956–57. It opened at the Théâtre Antoine in 1956 with Jeanne Moreau as Maggie. Coco Chanel designed the costumes.

30   Also cited in Peter Hall's 1988 program for *Orpheus Descending*.

31   For an attempt at an analysis of this transatlantic relationship, see Michael Billington's assessment in 2000, as he suggests, finally, "I suspect we have often misunderstood Williams in Britain." His references to productions of *Baby Doll* at the Albery Theatre and the National's revival of *Not about Nightingales* could have been folded into this analysis had space permitted: https://www.theguardian.com/culture/2000/jun/21/artsfeatures.stage.

32   https://www.standard.co.uk/go/london/theatre/scarlett-johansson-triumphs-in-cat-on-a-hot-tin-roof-and-vows-to-be-back-in-londons-west-end-8456770.html.

33   https://www.youngvic.org/whats-on/cat-on-a-hot-tin-roof   and   https://www.youtube.com/watch?v=LElE8KG3IZw.

34   See the full range of reviews at: http://ntlive.nationaltheatre.org.uk/productions/ntlout7-a-streetcar-named-desire.

Chapter 3 Becoming Samuel Beckett: Tennessee Williams and Theatrical Change on the Post–World War II World Stage

1   Reprinted in Bray, 2007, "Chapter Two: The Late Plays," 23–42.

2   One measure of *Iguana*'s popularity is its publication in full in the popular monthly magazine *Esquire* in February 1962, pp. 48–62. The publication carried the usual disclaimer for theatrical works: "This is the author's original [i.e., 1961] working

script and is subject to production changes." The book version appeared from New Directions in the spring.

3 Concluding his review in the *New York Times* on January 15, 1963, Howard Taubman was slightly more sympathetic: "A terrified comic ferocity courses through 'Milk Train' but the play generates little pity. By the standards of other lesser playwrights this is impressive work. By Mr. Williams' criteria it is disappointing because its resolution is hard to credit."

4 Tennessee Williams, foreword to *Memoirs* (New York: Doubleday, 1975), p. xvii.

5 In April of 1952 Quintero had directed Williams's *Summer and Smoke* at the fledgling Circle in the Square Theater. The theater and production helped launch the off-Broadway movement, and the production featured Geraldine Page as Alma. The play ran for over a year. Williams wrote in a notebook entry dated Tuesday, June 10, 1952: "The village [i. e. New York's Greenwich Village] success of 'Summer & Smoke' best thing that I've had this year" (Williams, 2006, 551). Williams hoped the actress and director could repeat their success with *Clothes for a Summer Hotel* in 1980.

6 Vidal on CBS broadcast, "The Homosexuals," 1967 (http://www.edgeboston.com/index.php?ch=columnists&sc=ryanshattuck&sc3=&id=117820&pg=3).

7 The pre-Broadway engagement of *Orpheus* was called *Something Wild in the Country* when it opened at the Shubert Theatre in Washington, DC, on February 21, 1957, with another tryout in Philadelphia on March 21, 1956, before opening at the Martin Beck Theatre in New York City for a disappointing run of 68 performances. It starred Maureen Stapleton and Robert Loggia, who was replaced by Cliff Robertson. *Something Wild in the Country* had been the working title for Tennessee Williams's first full-length play that opened and closed in Boston in 1940 as *Battle of Angels*. Original music for *Something Wild in the Country* was composed by Chuck Wayne, with the song "Heavenly Grass" composed by Paul Bowles with lyrics by Williams. Sets were by Boris Aronson and costumes by Lucinda Ballard. It was directed by Harold Clurman and produced by Robert Whitehead for the Producers Theatre.

8 Despite the reservations Williams has generally expressed toward the director, Clurman would go on to edit and write the introduction to *Tennessee Williams: Eight Plays*, published by Nelson Doubleday, Inc. It was reprinted in its Book Club Edition and again in a special edition by the International Collector's Library of Garden City, New York, a Doubleday subsidiary, all in 1979.

9 For a 2016 discussion of the relationship between *Suddenly, Last Summer* and the dismemberment of Pentheus in Euripides's *The Bacchae* offered by the Center for Hellenic Studies, see https://www.youtube.com/watch?v=eNYGME00P_0.

10 Williams could be quite disparaging about the play as well, especially in its earlier version. Asked by William Burroughs in 1977 where he wrote *Vieux Carré*, he answered in an interview published in the *Village Voice* (May 16): "I wrote *Vieux Carré* on a ship called the Oronza. My agent booked me out, after a play called *Out Cry*—some people called it *Out Rage*; in its longest form it was rather an outrage, of tedium" (Lotringer, 2001, 378, also cited in Devlin, 302). And again in 1979: "What most plays need is cutting. *Out Cry* was deplorably long. That's what was most dangerous to it. When I wrote it in 1967, I was crazy [.] I didn't know where I was. When you're really crazy you do some of your best work" (cited in Devlin, 308).

11 See S. E. Gontarski, "'I Think This Does Call for a Firm Stand': Beckett at the Royal Court," in *Beckett Matters: Essays on Beckett's Late Modernism* (Edinburgh: Edinburgh UP, 2016), pp. 255–72.

Chapter 4 Reframing Tennessee: A Short Afterword

1   https://www.irishtimes.com/culture/stage/endgame-by-samuel-beckett-life-conspires-to-mimic-art-yet-again-1.4276646.

2   See, for example, the group's production web site: http://www.complicite.org/productions/Endgame.

3   See a complete history of the decade-long writing process of *The Two-Character Play* in Saddik, 17n15. Saddik associates the play with "Williams' *Guignol*" experiment, a group of short plays whose "intention is to shock and so I call them my *Guignol*," as Williams wrote in a note on the Ts. (17).

4   Vol. 64, no. 2 (August 1, 1965), pp. 95–102, 130–34.

5   Vol. 66, no. 23 (June 13, 1969), pp. 11–12.

6   See Saddik (2015, 14–17) for a summary of such attacks.

7   For a catalogue of sordid details, see Michael Paller (2000).

8   Cited on the New Directions web page: https://www.ndbooks.com/author/tennessee-williams/#/.

9   Cohn cites the 1980 rather than the 1991 edition in her bibliography, although the 1991 edition is that listed in the volume's bibliography.

10   With STREETCAR, Tennessee has printed a license to speak at full throat, and it helped strengthen me as I turned to Willy Loman, a salesman always full of words, and better yet, a man who could never cease trying, like Adam, to name himself and the world's wonders. I had known all along that this play [*Death of a Salesman*] was not to be encompassed by conventional realism: and for one integral reason: in Willy the past was as alive as what was happening at the moment, sometimes even crashing in to completely overwhelm his mind. I wanted precisely the same fluidity in the form, and now it was clear to me that this must be primarily verbal. The language would of course have to be recognizably his to begin with, but it now [after *Streetcar*] seemed possible to infiltrate it with a kind of superconsciousness. (*Timebends*, 182)

11   http://www.tennesseewilliamsstudies.org/journal/work.php?ID=154.

12   https://www.maboumines.org/production/glass-guignol-the-brother-and-sister-play/.

13   Reviewer Carvajal, Doreen (or the caption writer for the *International Herald Tribune*) seemed confused by Breuer's comment on chronology, since one photo caption suggests, "But the setting is Japan, not the antebellum south." *Streetcar* is set in the antebellum south, we might add, only in Blanche's mind.

14   In some editions misprinted as "tight."

15   "Blanchett's Blanche pours life into a new production of Tennessee Williams's classic." See Ed Pilkington's review: https://www.theguardian.com/stage/2009/dec/03/cate-blanchett-a-streetcar-named-desire.

16   Five plays by Tennessee Williams: "The Dark Room," "Ten Blocks on the Camino Real," "The Case of the Crushed Petunias," "The Unsatisfactory Supper," and "Moony's Kid Don't Cry," published in an acting edition by Dramatists Play Service, Inc., 1948, reprinted in 1962, 1968, 1978, and 1990.

BIBLIOGRAPHY

Adams, Guy. "The Problem with Tennessee: Too Hot and Too Cool: A New Exhibition Reveals the American Playwright's Battles to Stage His Plays in Post-War London." *The Independent*, March 13, 2011. http://www.independent.co.uk/news/world/americas/the-problem-with-tennessee-too-hot-and-too-cool-2240490.html. Accessed March 4, 2021.

Anonymous. "Play Must Have Lines Taken Out." *Boston Post*, January 7, 1941, pp. 1, 8. Rpt. in *The Critical Response to Tennessee Williams*, ed. George W. Crandell. Westport, CT: Greenwood Press, 1996, p. 2.

Arrell, Doug. "Homophobic Criticism and Its Disguises: The Case of Stanley Kauffmann." *Journal of Dramatic Theory and Criticism* vol. 16, no. 2 (Spring 2002), pp. 95–110.

Atkinson, Brooks. "Theater: 2 by Williams." *New York Times*, January 2, 1958. https://archive.nytimes.com/www.nytimes.com/books/00/12/31/specials/williams-summer.html.

———. "The Play." *New York Times*, September 8, 1928. https://www.nytimes.com/1928/09/08/archives/the-play.html.

———. "Tobacco Road." Rpt. in The New York Times *Book of Broadway: On the Aisle for the Unforgettable Plays of the Last Century*, ed. Ben Brantley. New York: St. Martin's Press, 2001, pp. 85–86.

Bak, J. S. "Criticism on *A Streetcar Named Desire*: A Bibliographic Survey, 1947–2003." *Cercles* 10 (2004), pp. 3–32. http://www.cercles.com/n10/bak.pdf. Accessed March 4, 2021

"*Battle of Angels*." Provincetown Tennessee Williams Theater Festival. September 24–27, 2020. http://twptown.org/battle-of-angels. Accessed March 4, 2021.

Baxley, Barbara. "Barbara Baxley Papers, the Billy Rose Theatre Division at the New York Public Library for the Performing Arts," 2011. http://archives.nypl.org/the/18640. Accessed March 4, 2021.

Benedict, David. "Theatre/Tennessee Williams and His Women." *The Independent*, Wednesday, June 15, 1994.

"Becoming Tennessee Williams." *Harry Ransom Center*, February 1, 2011–July 31, 2011. https://www.hrc.utexas.edu/exhibitions/2011/becoming-tennessee-williams/. Accessed March 4, 2021.

Bertolini, Diana. "A Disturbed Genius Seen through the Eyes of an Intimate Friend: William Inge and Barbara Baxley." *New York Public Library: Archives*, June 28, 2013. Billy Rose Theatre Division, New York Public Library for the Performing Arts, Dorothy and Lewis B. Cullman Center. https://www.nypl.org/blog/2013/06/28/william-inge-barbara-baxley. Accessed March 4, 2021.

Billington, Michael. "*Cat on a Hot Tin Roof*." Theatre, *The Guardian*, December 1, 2009. https://www.theguardian.com/stage/2009/dec/02/cat-on-a-hot-tin-roof-billington.

————. "*Cat on a Hot Tin Roof*: Tennessee Williams's Southern Discomfort." *The Guardian*, December 30, 2012. https://www.theguardian.com/stage/2012/sep/30/cat-on-a-hot-tin-roof.

————. "*A Streetcar Named Desire* Review—Gillian Anderson Gives Stellar Performance." Culture, *The Guardian*, July 28, 2014. https://www.theguardian.com/stage/2014/jul/29/streetcar-named-desire-gillian-anderson-young-vic-review.

Bloom, Harold, ed. *Tennessee Williams's "A Streetcar Named Desire."* New York: Chelsea House, 1988.

Brantley, Ben, ed. The New York Times *Book of Broadway: On the Aisle for the Unforgettable Plays of the Last Century*. New York: St. Martin's Press, 2001.

————. "Hey, Stella! You Want to Banter?." *New York Times*, April 22, 2012. https://www.nytimes.com/2012/04/23/theater/reviews/a-streetcar-named-desire-at-the-broadhurst-theater.html.

————. "Brother, Can You Spare My Sanity." *New York Times*, June 21, 2013. https://www.nytimes.com/2013/06/22/theater/reviews/amanda-plummer-and-brad-dourif-in-tennessee-williams-rarity.html.

Bray, Robert, ed. "The Late Plays." In *Tennessee Williams and His Contemporaries*. Cambridge: Cambridge Scholars, 2007, pp. 23–42.

————, moderator. "Looking at the Late Plays of Tennessee Williams." *Tennessee Williams Annual Review* no. 5 (November 2002), p. 2. http://www.tennesseewilliamsstudies.org/archives/2002/1panel_lateplays.htm. Accessed March 4, 2021.

Brown, Martin. "Dear Tennessee Williams … Peter Brook's Letters Acquired by the V&A." *The Guardian*, September 25, 2014. https://www.theguardian.com/stage/2014/sep/25/peter-brook-victoria-and-albert-archives-purchased-stage.

Brustein, Robert Sanford. "The Men-Taming Women of William Inge." *Harpers Magazine*, November 1958, pp. 52–57. https://harpers.org/archive/1958/11/the-men-taming-women-of-william-inge/.

Carvajal, Doreen. "Mr. Molière, Meet Stanley Kowalski." *New York Times*. September 10, 2010. https://www.nytimes.com/2010/09/11/arts/11iht-plays.html. Excerpted at: https://www.maboumines.org/production/a-streetcar-named-desire/.

"'Cat on a Hot Tin Roof' Beats the Censor." 1957–58. http://www.overthefootlights.co.uk/1957-58.pdf. Accessed March 4, 2021.

Ciba, Daniel. "Dismembering Tennessee Williams: The Global Context of Lee Breuer's *A Streetcar Named Desire*." *Theatre Symposium* vol. 25 (2017), pp. 64–81. *Project MUSE*, doi:10.1353/tsy.2017.0005.

Clericuzio, Alessandro. "Tennessee Williams and Luchino Visconti: Various Stages of Outrage—and Censorship." *RSA Journal* vol. 25 (2014), pp. 35–58.

————. *Tennessee Williams and Italy: A Transcultural Perspective*. London: Palgrave Macmillan, 2016.

Clum, John M. *Still Acting Gay: Male Homosexuality in Modern Drama*. London: Palgrave Macmillan, [1991] 2001.

Cohn, Ruby. "Tennessee Williams: The Last Two Decades," *The Cambridge Companion to Tennessee Williams*, ed. Matthew C. Roudané, Cambridge: Cambridge University Press, 1997.

Corrigan, Mary Ann. "Realism and Theatricalism in *A Streetcar Named Desire*." *Modern Drama* vol. 19, no. 4 (Winter 1976), pp. 385–96.

Cosgrove, Ben. "Brando Takes Broadway: Life on the Set of 'A Streetcar Named desire' in 1947." *Life Magazine*. Arts and Entertainment, 1947, online: https://www.life.com/arts-entertainment/brando-takes-broadway-life-on-the-set-of-a-streetcar-named-desire-in-1947/.

Crandell, George W., ed. *The Critical Response to Tennessee Williams*. Westport, CT: Greenwood Press, 1996.

Crowther, Bosley. "Ford's Screen Version of 'Tobacco Road' at Roxy—'Mr. and Mrs. Smith' and Marx Brothers Here." *New York Times*. February 1941. https://www.nytimes.com/1941/02/21/archives/fords-screen-version-of-tobacco-road-at-roxy-mr-and-mrs-smith-and.html.

Devlin, Albert, ed. *Conversations with Tennessee Williams*. Jackson: University Press of Mississippi, 1986.

Dubois, Félicie. *Tennessee williams: l'oiseau sans pattes*. Paris: Balland, 1992.

Enelow, Shonni. "Sweating Tennessee Williams: Working Actors in *A Streetcar Named Desire* and *Portrait of a Madonna*." *Modern Drama* vol. 62, no. 2 (Summer 2019), pp. 129–48.

Evans, Greg. "The Red Devil Battery Sign." *Variety*, November 17, 1996. https://variety.com/1996/film/reviews/the-red-devil-battery-sign-1117911471/.

Fisher, James. "'The Angels of Fructification': Tennessee Williams, Tony Kushner, and Images of Homosexuality on the American Stage." *Mississippi Quarterly*, vol. 49, no. 1 (Winter 1995–96), pp. 13–32.

Freedman, Samuel G. "A Playwright's Early Works Offer Glimpses of His Later Genius." *New York Times*, May 18, 1986. https://www.nytimes.com/1986/05/18/theater/a-playwright-s-early-works-offer-glimpses-of-his-later-genius.html.

Garner, Dwight. "Pulp Valentine: Erskine Caldwell's Lurid Vision of the American South." *Slate*, May 24, 2006. http://www.slate.com/articles/news_and_politics/pulp_fiction/2006/05/pulp_valentine_2.html.

Gindt, Dirk. "When Broadway Came to Sweden: The European Premiere of Tennessee Williams's *Cat on a Hot Tin Roof*." *Theatre Survey* vol. 53, no. 1 (2012), pp. 59–83.

———. "Transatlantic Translations and Transactions: Lars Schmidt and the Implementation of Postwar American Theatre in Europe." *Theatre Journal* vol. 65, no.1 (2013), pp. 19–37. Rpt at: https://www.loc.gov/collections/lars-schmidt/articles-and-essays/implementation-of-postwar-american-theatre-in-europe/. Accessed March 4, 2021.

———. *Tennessee Williams in Sweden and France, 1945–1965: Cultural Translations, Sexual Anxieties and Racial Fantasies*. London: Bloomsbury, 2019.

Goldthwaite, Charles A., Jr. "All Shook Up: Elvis, Bo, and the White Negro in Tennessee Williams's *Orpheus Descending*." *Tennessee Williams Annual Review*, no. 8 (November 2006), p. 2. http://www.tennesseewilliamsstudies.org/journal/work.php?ID=70. Accessed March 4, 2021.

Gontarski, S. E., ed. *Un tram che si chiama desiderio / A Streetcar Named Desire*. Canone teatrale europeo / Canon of European Drama. No. 7. A cura di / edited by S. E. Gontarski. Pisa, Italia: Edizioni ETS, 2012.

Goska, Danusha V. "The Bohunk in American Cinema." *Journal of Popular Culture* vol. 39, no. 3 (2006), pp. 407–29.

Grissom, James (2013). "Notes on William Inge's *Picnic*: The Force of Identity." January 13, 2013. http://jamesgrissom.blogspot.com/2013/01/notes-on-william-inges-picnic-force-of.html. Accessed March 4, 2021.

———. *Follies of God*: *Tennessee Williams and the Women of the Fog*, New York: Alfred A. Knopf, 2015.

Gunn, Drewey Wayne. *Tennessee Williams: A Bibliography*. Metuchen, NJ: Scarecrow Press, 1991.

Heintzelman, Greta, and Alycia Smith-Howard. *Critical Companion to Tennessee Williams*. New York: Facts on File, 2005.

"Homosexuality, Censorship and the British Stage." *British Library Blog*, June 27, 2019. https://blogs.bl.uk/untoldlives/2019/06/homosexuality-censorship-and-the-british-stage.html. Accessed March 4, 2021.

Hooper, M. "There Will Be Pity for the Wild." In *Sexual Politics in the Work of Tennessee Williams: Desire over Protest*. Cambridge: Cambridge University Press, 2012, pp. 70–123.

Hope-Wallace, Philip. "*Cat on a Hot Tin Roof* Evades Censors." *The Guardian*, January 31, 1958. https://www.theguardian.com/theguardian/2013/jan/31/tennesseewilliams-theatre.

Howe, Benjamin Ryder, Jeanne McCullock and Mona Simpson. "Sam Shepard: The Art of Theater No. 12." *Paris Review*, no. 142 (Spring 1997). https://www.theparisreview.org/interviews/1281/sam-shepard-the-art-of-theater-no-12-sam-shepard. Accessed March 4, 2021.

Isaacs, Edith J. R., ed. *Theatre Arts Monthly* vol. 12, no. 10 (October 1928).

Izard, Barbara, and Clara Hieronymus. "*Requiem for a Nun: On Stage and Off*." Nashville, TN: Aurora, 1970.

"Jockey: Our Story." https://www.jockey.com/ourcompany/ourhistory. Accessed March 4, 2021.

Kaplan, David, ed. *Tenn at One Hundred: The Reputation of Tennessee Williams*. East Brunswick, NJ: Hansen, 2011.

Kauffmann, Stanley. "Homosexual Drama and Its Disguises." *New York Times*, January 23, 1966, section 2, p. 1.

———. "On the Acceptability of the Homosexual," *New York Times*, February 6, 1966, section 2, p. i.

Kazan, Elia. "Notebook for *A Streetcar Named Desire*." In *Directors on Directing*, ed. Toby Cole and Helen C. Chinoy, rev. ed. Indianapolis: Bobbs-Merrill, 1963, pp. 364–73.

Kennedy, Pagan. "Who Made That T-Shirt?" *New York Times Magazine*, September 20, 2013. https://www.nytimes.com/2013/09/22/magazine/who-made-that-t-shirt.html. Accessed March 4, 2021.

Kolin, Philip C. "[A Letter from Sir Laurence] Olivier to Williams: An Introduction." *Missouri Review* vol. 13, no. 2 (1991), pp. 141–50.

———. "The First Critical Assessments of *A Streetcar Named Desire*: The *Streetcar* Tryouts and the Reviewers." *Journal of Dramatic Criticism and Theory* vol. 6, no. 1 (Fall 1991), pp. 45–67. (Reprints pre-Broadway reviews.)

———. *Tennessee Williams: A Guide to Research and Performance*. Westport, CT: Greenwood Press, 1998, p. 104.

———. *Williams: A Streetcar Named Desire* (Plays in Production). Cambridge: Cambridge University Press, 2000.

———. "Polish Language and History in *A Streetcar Named Desire*." *Notes on Contemporary Literature* vol. 41, no. 3 (2011). *Gale Academic OneFile*. https://go.gale.com/ps/anonymous?id=GALE%7CA274115299&sid=googleScholar&v=2.1&it=r&linkaccess=abs&issn=00294047&p=AONE&sw=w. Accessed September 30, 2020.

Kontaxopoulos, Jean. "Orpheus Introspecting: Tennessee Williams and Jean Cocteau." *Tennessee Williams Annual Review*, no. 4 (2001), pp. 1–26.

Kuchwara, Michael. "*Orpheus Descending*, Starring Vanessa Redgrave, Opens on Broadway." Associated Press, September 25, 1989. http://www.apnewsarchive.com/1989/-Orpheus-Descending-Starring-Vanessa-Redgrave-Opens-on-Broadway/id-4c8af884cd33406e9ad52a24ff804dff. Accessed March 4, 2021.

Lahr, John. *Tennessee Williams: Mad Pilgrimage of the Flesh*, New York: W. W. Norton, 2014.

Levy, Alan. "The Long Wait for Godot." *Theatre Arts* vol. 40, no. 8 (August 1956), pp. 33–35, 96.

Londré, Felicia Hardison. "The Two Character Out Cry and Break Out." In *The Undiscovered Country: The Later Plays of Tennessee Williams*, ed. Philip C. Colin. New York: Peter Lang, 2002.

Loomis, Jeffrey B. "Dialogues of Dueling Genres: Williams's *Streetcar* and *Rose Tattoo*." In *Texts & Presentations*, ed. Graley Herren. Jefferson, NC: McFarland, 2016, pp. 158–74.

Lord Chamberlain's Report, *Cat on a Hot Tin Roof* (file LPC CORR 1964/4496). Documents held by the British Library and quotations cited via Creative Commons Non-Commercial License and the British Open Government License.

Lotringer, Sylvère, ed. "Orpheus Holds His Own." In *Burroughs Live: The Collected Interviews of William S. Burroughs, 1960–1997* (Double Agent). New York: Semiotext(e), 2001, pp. 376–83.

MacClintock, Lander. "A Decade of American Theatre in Italy: 1940-1950." *Italica*, vol. 30, no. 2 (1953), pp. 90–109. *JSTOR*, www.jstor.org/stable/477475. Accessed April 9, 2021.

Mcmillan, Gloria Lee. "Variation drawings for *Streetcar Named Desire* Opera." 2020. https://www.researchgate.net/publication/341358415_Variation_drawings_for_Streetcar_named_Desire_Opera. Accessed March 4, 2021.

Maruejouls-Koch, Sophie. "The Haunted Stage of *Summer and Smoke*." *Modern Drama* vol. 57, no. 1 (Spring 2017), pp. 19–40.

Miller, Dan B. *Erskine Caldwell: The Journey from Tobacco Road*. New York: Alfred A. Knopf, 1995.

Montgomery, Paul N. "William Inge, Playwright, Is Dead." *New York Times*, June 11, 1973. https://www.nytimes.com/1973/06/11/archives/william-inge-playwright-is-dead-william-inge-who-won-53-pulitzer.html.

Murphy, Brenda. *The Theatre of Tennessee Williams*, London: Bloomsbury/Methuen, 2014.

O'Connor, Jacqueline. *Law and Sexuality in Tennessee Williams's America*. Teaneck, NJ: Fairleigh Dickinson University Press, 2016.

Olivier Archive, British Library, vol. CCLXIX (ff.). *A Streetcar Named Desire* by Tennessee Williams; produced by Olivier for Tennant Productions, starring Vivien Leigh as Blanche Dubois. First performance at the Aldwych; October 11, 1949.1. ff. Add MS 80034: 1949–90. http://hviewer.bl.uk/IamsHViewer/Default.aspx?mdark=ark:/81055/vdc_100000001514.0x0001e0&_ga=2.26956989.1875097185.1618233903-1198399574.1618233903.

Paglia, Camille. "Tennessee Williams and *A Streetcar Named Desire*." In *Provocations: Collected Essays on Art, Feminism, Politics, Sex, and Education*. New York: Pantheon, 2018, pp. 233–39.

———. "Tennessee Williams." In *A New Literary History of America*, ed. Greil Marcus and Werner Sollors, Cambridge, MA: Harvard University Press Reference Library, 2012. http://www.newliteraryhistory.com/tennesseewilliams.html. Accessed March 4, 2021.

Paller, Michael. "The Couch and Tennessee." *Tennessee Williams Annual Review*, no. 3 (2000). http://www.tennesseewilliamsstudies.org/journal/work.php?ID=29. Accessed March 4, 2021.

———. *Gentlemen Callers: Tennessee Williams, Homosexuality, and Mid-Twentieth Century Drama*. London: Palgrave Macmillan, 2005.

Palmer, R. Barton (Moderator). "A Black *Cat* and Other Plays: African American Productions of Williams's Drama." *Tennessee Williams Annual Review*, 2011.

Palmer, R. Barton, and William Robert Bray. *Hollywood's Tennessee: The Williams Films and Postwar America*, Austin: University of Texas Press, 2009.

Parker, Brian. "Bring Back Big Daddy." *Tennessee Williams Annual Review*, no. 3 (2000). http://www.tennesseewilliamsstudies.org/journal/work.php?ID=32. Accessed March 4, 2021.

Prosser, William. *The Late Plays of Tennessee Williams*. Lanham, MD: Scarecrow Press, 2008.

Rich, Frank. "In London, Taking Williams Seriously," *New York Times*, section C, December 15, 1988, p. 15. https://www.nytimes.com/1988/12/15/theater/review-theater-in-london-taking-williams-seriously.html.

———. "Review/Theater; Vanessa Redgrave in 'Orpheus': Matching Artistic Sensibilities." *New York Times*, September 25, 1989. https://www.nytimes.com/1989/09/25/theater/review-theater-vanessa-redgrave-in-orpheus-matching-artistic-sensibilities.html.

Rogoff, Gordon, "The Fugitive Play." In *Vanishing Acts: Theatre since the Sixties*, New Haven, CT: Yale University Press, 2000.

Roudané, Matthew C., ed. *The Cambridge Companion to Tennessee Williams*. Cambridge: Cambridge University Press, 1997.

Robinson, James A. "The Masculine Primitive and 'The Hairy Ape.'" *Eugene O'Neill Review* vol. 19, nos. 1/2 (Spring/Fall 1995), pp. 95–109. https://www.jstor.org/stable/29784551?seq=1#page_scan_tab_contents.

Saddik, Annette J. "Critical Expectations and Assumptions: Williams' Later Reputation and the American Reception of the Avant-Garde." In *Tennessee Williams*, ed. Harold Bloom. New York: Infobase, 2009. (Rpt. from Saddik 1999.)

———. *The Politics of Reputation: The Critical Reception of Tennessee Williams' Later Plays*. Madison, NJ: Fairleigh Dickinson University Press, 1999.

———. *Tennessee Williams and the Theatre of Excess: The Strange, the Crazed, the Queer*, Cambridge: Cambridge University Press, 2015.

Savran, David. *Communists, Cowboys, and Queers: The Politics of Masculinity in the Work of Arthur Miller and Tennessee Williams*. Minneapolis, MN: University of Minnesota Press, 1992.

———. "The Kindness of Strangers? Tennessee Williams in France and Germany." In *Tennessee Williams and Europe*, ed. Jon S. Bak. DQR Studies in Literature Online, Volume 54. Leiden: Brill/Rodopi, 2014. https://brill.com/view/book/edcoll/9789401211277/B9789401211277-s013.xml.

Schulman, Michael. "Theater Can't Miss This Moment: An Interview with Audra McDonald." *New Yorker*, July 26, 2020. https://www.newyorker.com/culture/the-new-yorker-interview/theatre-cant-miss-this-moment-an-interview-with-audra-mcdonald.

Staggs, Sam. *When Blanche Met Brando: The Scandalous Story of "A Streetcar Named Desire."* New York: St Martin's Griffin, 2006. (The cover photo features a tastelessly pj'd Brando in mid assault on Blanche.)

———. "A Night to Go Down in History: The Premiere of *A Streetcar Named Desire*." In *Tenn at One Hundred: The Reputation of Tennessee Williams*, ed. David Kaplan. East Brunswick, NJ: Hansen, 2011, pp. 79–84.

St. Just, Maria. *Five O'Clock Angel: Letters of Tennessee Williams to Maria St. Just, 1948–1982* (with commentary by Maria St. Just). New York: Alfred A. Knopf, 1990.

Shellard, Dominic. *Kenneth Tynan: A Life*. New Haven, CT: Yale University Press, 2003.

Spoto, Donald. *The Kindness of Strangers: The Life of Tennessee Williams*, New York: Little Brown, 1985.

Taylor, Paul, "First Night: *Cat on a Hot Tin Roof*, Novello Theatre, London." *Independent*, December 2, 2009. https://www.independent.co.uk/arts-entertainment/theatre-dance/reviews/first-night-cat-on-a-hot-tin-roof-novello-theatre-london-1832341.html.

Van Duyvenbode, R. "Darkness Made Visible: Miscegenation, Masquerade and the Signified Racial Other in Tennessee Williams' *Baby Doll* and *A Streetcar Named Desire.*" *Journal of American Studies* vol. 35, no. 2 (2001), pp. 203–15. http://www.jstor.org/stable/27556964. Accessed September 30, 2020.

Voss, Ralph E., ed. *Magical Muse: Millennial Essays on Tennessee Williams*, Tuscaloosa: University of Alabama Press, 2015.

Williams, Tennessee. *27 Wagons Full of Cotton and Other One-Act Plays*, London: John Lehmann, 1949.

———. *A Streetcar Named Desire*. New York: A Signet Books, 1951.

———. "Florida Première for New Tennessee Williams Play." *Theatre Arts* vol. 40, no. 8 (August 1956), pp. 66–67. (Interview with photographs and play summary).

———. *Cat on a Hot Tin Roof*. New York: A Signet Book, 1958.

———. *Sweet Bird of Youth*. New York: A Signet Book, 1959.

———. Introduction to *Dark at the Top of the Stairs*. New York: Bantam Books, 1960, pp. vii–ix.

———. *The Fugitive Kind*. New York: A Signet Book, 1960.

———. *Suddenly, Last Summer*. New York: A Signet Book, 1960.

———. *Out Cry*. New York: New Directions Books, 1973. (To coincide with the 1973 production under that title.)

———. "To William Inge: An Homage." *New York Times*. July 1, 1973. https://www.nytimes.com/1973/07/01/archives/to-william-inge-an-homage-william-inge.html. Accessed September 30, 2020.

———. *Memoirs*. New York: Doubleday, 1975. (Reissued with an Introduction by John Waters. New York: New Directions Books, 2006.)

———. *The Two-Character Play*. New York: New Directions Books, 1975, revised edition January 17, 1979. [The latter is the text Williams selected for *The Theatre of Tennessee Williams*, Volume 5. The text for The Library of America anthology, however, whether by design or inattention, reprints the *Out Cry* text of 1973.]

———. *Clothes for a Summer Hotel: A Ghost Story*. New York: New Directions Books, 1983.

———. *Cat on a Hot Tin Roof*, Vivien Leigh's unannotated script. This mimeograph retyping reflects the cuts required by the Lord Chamberlain, Harry Ransom Humanities Research Center, University of Texas, Austin, TX. MS-04535, Box 43, Folder 9.

———. *The Selected Letters of Tennessee Williams, Volume I, 1920–1945*, ed. Albert J. Devlin and Nancy Marie Patterson Tischler. New York: New Directions Books, 2002.

———. *The Selected Letters of Tennessee Williams, Volume II, 1945–1957*, ed. Albert J. Devlin, co-edited with Nancy M. Tischler. New York: New Directions Books, 2004.

———. *Notebooks*, ed. Margaret Bradham Thorton. New Haven, CT: Yale University Press, 2007.

———. *Cat on a Hot Tin Roof* (student edition with Introduction and Notes), ed. Philip C. Kolin. London: Methuen, 2010, pp. lxii–lxiii.

Yates, Daniel B. "Gene David Kirk." *Exeunt Magazine*. March 28, 2011. http://exeuntmagazine.com/features/gene-on-tennessee/. Accessed September 30, 2020.

Zinoman, Jason, "Theater: Excerpt; *Cat on a Hot Tin Roof*." *New York Times*, November 2, 2003. https://www.nytimes.com/2003/11/02/theater/theater-excerpt-cat-on-a-hot-tin-roof.html.

INDEX

Adams, Guy 50
The Adding Machine (Rice) 20
African Americans 35–39, 41, 74
Albee, Edward 86–87
Allen, Debbie 34, 38–39
All That Fall (Beckett) 80
American National Theater and Academy
  (ANTA) 20
American Place Theatre 37
Anderson, Kevin 55
Andrews, Benedict 60
Ashford, Rob 59
Atkinson, Brooks 21, 24, 77
Auto-da-Fé (Williams) 10
Aylesworth, Reiko 73

Baley, Barbara 29
Barnes, Clive 72
Battle of Angels (Williams) 5–6, 17, 55,
  74, 78–79
Beaufort, John 66
Beckett, Samuel 4, 42, 50, 64, 73, 80–81,
  85–90, 97
Benedict, David 69
Benton, Thomas Hart 19
Bergman, Ingmar 64
Bertolini, Diana 29
Beyond the Horizon (O'Neill) 18
Billington, Michael 39, 48–49
Black Lives Matter 38
Bound East for Cardiff (O'Neill) 18
Bowles, Paul 46
Brando, Marlon 15–18, 55
Brantley, Ben 35, 79, 88
Bray, Robert 62–64
Breath (Beckett) 87
Breuer, Lee 90–91

Broadway productions 25, 39, 46, 56, 58
Broadway theater 37–38
Brook, Peter 57
Broström, Gunnel 45
Brown, Phil 46
Bruccoli, Matthew J. 66
Brustein, Robert 29
buttonless undershirt 13
Byrd, Stephen C. 34

Caldwell, Erskine 24–26
Callahan, Dan 67–68
Camino Real (Williams) 21, 27, 42, 67,
  81, 89, 97
Camus, Albert 26
Canning, Charlotte 6
Canzanella, Danilo 78
Cat on a Hot Tin Roof (Williams) 4, 25,
  33–34, 38, 41–50, 55–60, 65, 81
A Cavalier for Milady (Williams) 80
censorship 6, 15, 31, 43–47
Charleson, Ian 34
Chekhov, Anton 12
Chevara, Robert 80
Clericuzio, Alessandro 81–82
Clothes for a Summer Hotel: A Ghost Play
  (Williams) 30, 65, 66, 68–72, 83
Clurman, Harold 20, 56
Cocteau, Jean 64
Cohn, Ruby 83, 88–89
Colleano, Bonar 18
color-blind casting 39–40
Come Back, Little Sheba (Inge) 27
A Comedy of Errors (Shakespeare) 39
Cool Hand Luke (1967) 30
Crandell, George 36
Crawford, Cheryl 20

Crawford, Joan 6
Critical Companion to Tennessee Williams
    73, 89
Critical Race Theory (CRT) 38
Crowther, Bosley 24
cultural friction/resistance 54–58

Dakin, Walter E. 4
D'Amico, Masolino 59, 76
The Dark at the Top of the Stairs
    (Williams) 25, 29
Davies, Howard 34, 49, 59
Dean, James 9, 30
De Capitani, Elio 59, 76–78, 81
Deleuze, Gilles 85
Déprats, Jean-Michel 90–91
Designated Mourner (Shawn) 88
Desire under the Elms (O'Neill) 20
Dorff, Linda 62
Dourif, Brad 79
DuBois, Blanche 3, 6, 12–13, 15–18,
    21–22
Duncan, Lindsay 34
Duyvenbode, Rachel Van 35

East of Eden (Kazan, 1953) 30
Endgame (Beckett) 81, 85–86
*Erskine Caldwell: The Journey from Tobacco
    Road* (Miller) 25
Evans, Greg 87–88

fashion 9–10
Faulkner, William 29–30
Finley, Boss 37
Fitzgerald, F. Scott 10, 66
Fitzgerald, Zelda 30, 66
The Flowering Peach (Odets) 25
Ford, John 24
Fraysse, Caroline Kellet 42
Free Man of Color (Guare) 41
"free people of color" 41
friendship 4
The Fugitive Kind (1960, Williams) 16–17,
    28–29, 55, 79

Game, H. C. 52
The Garden District (Williams) 76
Garner, Dwight 25–26

Gassner, John 5
Gazzara, Ben 25
Geddes, Barbara Bel 25, 55
Giammarini, Cristian 76
Giant (1956) 30
Gielgud, John 46
Glass Guignol: The Brother and Sister Play 90
The Glass Menagerie (Williams) 1–2, 4–6, 26,
    33, 46–47, 62, 80–81, 94, 96
God's Little Acre (Caldwell) 25
Goldthwaite, Charles A., Jr. 74
González, Rodríguez y 13
Gordone, Charles 39
Goska, Danusha V. 35
Gothenburg production 46
The Great Ziegfeld 2–3
Guare, John 41
Guerrieri, Gerardo 76
Gwatkin, N. W. 50–51

Haight, Kenneth 66
Hair (1967) 64
The Hairy Ape (O'Neill) 18
Hall, Peter 34, 46, 49–50, 59–60, 73–75,
    79, 81, 89
Hammett, Dashiell 10
Hands, Ciaran 59
Harry Ransom Humanities Research
    Center at the University of Texas 6
Hayes, Helen 46
Hays, Will 30
Hays Commission (1934–54) 30
Heflin, Frances 46
Heintzelman, Greta 73, 89
Hemingway, Ernest 65
Heriot, C. D. 44–45
Hill, George Roy 65
Hobson, Harold 54
homosexuality 4, 18, 23, 50, 54, 57–58,
    68, 77, 81
Hope-Wallace, Philip 43
Hopper, Hedda 65
Howard, Terrence 34
Hud (1963) 30
Hughie (O'Neill) 17
The Hustler (1961) 30
hyperfemininity 18
hypermasculinity 4, 10, 18

Improvvisamente, l'estate scorsa (Williams) (2011) 59
Independent 39
Inge, William 9–32
In the Bar of a Tokyo Hotel (Williams) 72–73, 79–81, 87, 89
Islands in the Stream (Hemingway) 68
Italian Americans 37

Jenkins, Anne 44
Jim Crow laws 37
Jones, Alia M. 34
Jones, James Earl 34

Kanfer, Stefan 87
Kauffman, Stanley 69
Kazan, Elia 21, 25, 27–28, 31, 34, 44–45, 48–49, 55–57, 59, 97
Kerr, Walter 66, 68
Killeen, Terence 85
Kirk, David 80–81, 83
Kirkland, Jack 24
Kolin, Philip C. 7, 35–37, 62–63
Kowalski, Stanley 14–16, 21, 30–31
Kowalski effect 10
Krapp's Last Tape (Beckett) 87
Kubie, Lawrence 54–55
Kuchwara, Michael 74

Lady Chatterley's Lover (Lawrence) 31
Lahr, John 14, 38
Langner, Lawrence 6
La Stampa 76
The Last Tycoon (Fitzgerald) 66
Leigh, Vivien 18
Levy, Alan 74
The Long Goodby 5
The Long Hot Summer (1958, Faulkner) 29–30
Look Back in Anger (Osborne) 46, 103n14
Loomis, Jeffrey B. 23–24
Lord Chamberlain 81
    blue pencil 50–58
    Endgame 81, 85–86
    office 44–46
Lumet, Sidney 55

Machinal (Treadwell) (1928) 21
Mailer, Norman 74

Malden, Karl 17
male undergarments vendors 10
Maltese Falcon (1930, 1941) 10, 17
Mann, Emily 34–35
masculinity 9–32, 97
    African-American 74
    hypermasculinity 4, 10, 18
    lower class 20
    mode of 15–16
    modernist 28
    queering of 28
    robust 20
    stretch T-shirt and 17
    Williams's images of postwar 9
Masks Outrageous and Austere (Williams) 102n5
McDermott, Hugh 46
McDonald, Audra 40
McIntyre, Ned 39
McMillan, Gloria 37
Memoirs (Williams) 5, 33, 58, 63
Merlo, Frank 64
Mielziner, Jo 46
The Milk Train Doesn't Stop Here Anymore (Williams) 64
Miller, Dan B. 25
modern drama 46–50
Montgomery, Paul L. 29

Nathan, George Jean 14
Newman, Paul 9, 25
Nicoll, Allardyce 52
The Night of the Iguana (Williams) 58, 64
non-normative sexuality 24
North, Alex 48
Nunn, Trevor 80

Ochello, Peter 4
Odets, Clifford 20, 25
O'Hara, Robert 40
Oh! Calcutta! (1969) 64
Olivier, Laurence 47–49, 64
O'Neill, Eugene 17–18, 20
Orpheus Descending (Williams) 6, 16, 46, 55, 57, 60, 74–76, 79, 89
Osborne, John 46
Out Cry (Williams) 30, 62–64, 73, 88–89

Pacino, Al 9
Page, Geraldine 25, 66
Parker, Nicole Ari 34
"The Passion of the Moth" 24
people of color 41–42
Period of Adjustment (Williams) 65
Picnic (Inge) 27
Pinter, Harold 4
Piscator, Erwin 26
Playbill 34
Plummer, Amanda 79
Poker Night (1948) 19
Polish-Americans 36
Pollitt, Brick 4
Post–World War II Theater Climate
    (London)
    cultural friction and resistance 54–58
    Lord Chamberlain's blue pencil 50–58
    Lord Chamberlain's office 44–46
    modern drama, start of 46–50
    theatrical change on world stage 61–83
power 28–29
*A Prayer for the Wild of Heart That Are Kept in
    Cages* (Williams) 21, 23
'The Primary Colors' 24

queer sexualities 8
Quick, Ben 29–30
Quintero, Jose 66
Quotations from Chairman Mao Tse Tung
    (Albee) 87

race 34–42
race neutral 38–39
Rachad, Phylicia 34
racial blindness 39–40
rape 22–23
Rasky, Harry 37
Rebel without a Cause (1955) 30
The Red Devil Battery Sign (Williams) 88
Redgrave, Venessa 55
Requiem for a Nun (Faulkner) 26
Rice, Elmer 21, 89, 98n11
Rich, Frank 33–34, 42, 49, 55, 60, 75, 79
Richardson, Tony 46
Robinson, James A. 20
Rockefeller Foundation 5
Rogoff, Gordon 62, 74
Rose, Anika Noni 34

The Rose Tattoo (Williams) 37, 45
Rubin-Vega, Daphne 34

Saddik, Annette J. 8, 62, 90
Sanctuary (Faulkner) (1931) 26
Sandbox (Albee) 87
Saroyan, William 74
Save Me the Waltz (Zelda Fitzgerald) 71
Savran, David 8
Schneider, Alan 74, 86
Schott Perfecto One Star motorcycle
    jacket 16
Schulman, Michael 40
self-reflexive theater 4
sexuality 2–4, 15, 17–18, 21, 23–24, 29,
    33, 35, 39, 46, 58, 64, 66–69,
    73, 77
sexual tensions 23
Shawn, Wallace 88
Shepard, Sam 9, 30–31
Sillcox, Luise M. 5
Slapstick Tragedy (Williams) 86
Smith-Howard, Alycia 73, 89
Something Unspoken 76–77
Something Wild in the Country 105n7
Southern Gothic 9
Spring Storm 5
Stairs to the Roof (Williams) 21, 100n10
Stapleton, Maureen 55
Stasburg, Lee 20
Strabler, Johnny 30
"The Strangest Kind of Romance" 12–13
Straw, Jack 4
A Streetcar Named Desire (Williams) 3–4, 6–7,
    10–12, 14, 16–17, 19, 23, 26, 30,
    33–40, 43, 45, 47, 50, 52, 54–55, 57,
    59–64, 75, 80–81, 86, 88, 90–96
Street Scene (Rice) 20
Suddenly, Last Summer (Williams) 25, 54–55,
    57, 76–78
Sweet Bird of Youth (Williams) 4, 25, 27, 37,
    45, 69, 73, 89, 96

Taylor, Elizabeth 25, 77
Taylor, Paul 39–40
Ten Blocks on the Camino Real (Williams) 21
Tennent, H. M. 50
*Tennessee Williams: A Portrait in Laughter and
    Lamentations* 37

Tennessee Williams and His Contemporaries 62–63
Tennessee Williams and the Theatre of Excess: The Strange, The Crazed, The Queer (Saddik) 8
Theater 1969 87
This Property Is Condemned (Williams) 5
This Side of Paradise (F. Scott Fitzgerald) (1920) 10
Tobacco Road (Caldwell) 24–26
Treadwell, Sophie 21
T-shirt modernism 4, 9–32
  advertisement 11–13, 30
  beneficiaries of 10
  buttonless undershirt 13
  described by DuBois, Blanche 21–22
  emergence 9–10
  Pacino era 30
  Williams's brand of 29–30
The Two-Character Play (Williams) 30, 62–64, 73, 79–80, 83, 86, 88–90
Tynan, Kenneth 49, 56

under-shirt 11
Underwood, Blair 34
unmentionables 11
Un tram che si chiama desiderio (Williams) (1995) 59

Varsouviana 35
Vidal, Gore 10, 14–15, 48, 63, 68, 77
Vincentelli, Elisabeth 72–73
Visconti, Luchino 64

Waiting for Godot (Beckett) 42, 46, 50, 73–74, 85, 87, 89
Waiting for Lefty (Odets) (1935) 20
Watergate Theatre Club 43
Wayne, Chance 3–4, 37
Who's Afraid of Virginia Woolf? (Albee) 86–87
Wilder, Thorton 74
The Wild One (1953) 16, 18, 30
Williams, Cornelius Coffin 4
Williams, Rose 1–2
Williams, Tennessee 1–8, 9–32, 33–60, 85–97
  anglicizing 42–58
  Auto-da-Fé 10
  Battle of Angels 17

birth 4
Camino Real of 1953 21
case studies 90–97
Cat on a Hot Tin Roof 4, 25, 33–34, 38, 41–50, 55–60, 65, 81
A Cavalier for Milady 80
Clothes for a Summer Hotel: A Ghost Play 30, 65–66, 68–72, 83
comedy 65
conflicts 39, 41
decline 64–65
depiction of women 68
education 5
family 4–5
The Fugitive Kind (1960) 16–17, 28–29, 55, 79
The Glass Menagerie 1–2, 4–6, 26, 33, 46–47, 62, 80–81, 94, 96
heroines 68
images of postwar masculinity 9
Masks Outrageous and Austere 102n5
Memoirs 5, 33, 58, 63
Orpheus Descending 6, 16–17, 46, 55, 57, 60, 74–76, 79, 89
Out Cry 30, 62–64, 73, 88–89
racialized 34–42
reframing of work 85–97
Rich's observation on 33–34
sexuality 2–4, 15, 17–18, 21, 23–24, 29, 33, 35, 39, 46, 58, 64, 66–69, 73, 77
sexually charged work 33–34, 68–69
Spring Storm 5
Stairs to the Roof 21, 100n10
"The Strangest Kind of Romance" 12–13
A Streetcar Named Desire 3–4, 6–7, 14, 16–17, 19, 23, 26, 30, 33–40, 43, 45, 47, 50, 52, 54–55, 57, 59–64, 75, 80–81, 86, 88, 90–96
Suddenly, Last Summer 25, 54–55, 57, 76–78
Sweet Bird of Youth 4, 25, 27, 37, 45, 69, 73, 89, 96
and theatrical change on Post–World War II world stage 61–83
The Two-Character Play 30, 62–64, 73, 79–80, 83, 86, 88–90
in United Kingdom 82–83
works 6–8
Wilson, August 38

Wilson, Edmund 66
Winfield, Tom 2
Wood, Audrey 5, 27
Woollcott, Alexander 18–19

Young, Harvey 34, 36

Ziegfeld Follies 2–3
Zinoman, Jason 56

Lightning Source UK Ltd.
Milton Keynes UK
UKHW012119220621
385966UK00001B/20

9 781785 276873